Digital Nomad

How to Become a Digital Nomad

(A Guide to Traveling and Working From Anywhere)

Richard Haber

Published By **Ryan Princeton**

Richard Haber

All Rights Reserved

Digital Nomad: How to Become a Digital Nomad (A Guide to Traveling and Working From Anywhere)

ISBN 978-1-77485-809-7

No part of this guidebook shall be reproduced in any form without permission in writing from the publisher except in the case of brief quotations embodied in critical articles or reviews.

Legal & Disclaimer

The information contained in this ebook is not designed to replace or take the place of any form of medicine or professional medical advice. The information in this ebook has been provided for educational & entertainment purposes only.

The information contained in this book has been compiled from sources deemed reliable, and it is accurate to the best of the Author's knowledge; however, the Author cannot guarantee its accuracy and validity and cannot be held liable for any errors or omissions. Changes are periodically made to this book. You must consult your doctor or get professional medical advice before using any of the suggested remedies, techniques, or information in this book.

Upon using the information contained in this book, you agree to hold harmless the Author from and against any damages, costs, and expenses, including any legal fees potentially resulting from the application of any of the information provided by this guide. This disclaimer applies to any damages or injury caused by the use and application, whether directly or indirectly, of any advice or information presented, whether for breach of contract, tort, negligence, personal injury, criminal intent, or under any other cause of action.

You agree to accept all risks of using the information presented inside this book. You need to consult a professional medical practitioner in order to ensure you are both able and healthy enough to participate in this program.

TABLE OF CONTEN

Introduction 1

Chapter 1: What Is It Mean To Be A Digital Nomad..................................5

Chapter 2: Becoming A Global Citizen Instead Of A Local Citizen 12

Chapter 3: Top Locations To Be An Digital Nomad..................................17

Chapter 4: Obtaining A Second Passport..28

Chapter 5: Essentials In Offshore Tax Planning..44

Chapter 6: What Is The Tax-Free Residence Program?......................51

Chapter 7: What To Do To Keep Your Money Safe In Offshore Banks 59

Chapter 8: Should I Utilize Off Shore Companies To Grow My Company?70

Chapter 9: Disconnecting From Matrix..84

Chapter 10: Adventure Or Escapism 95

Chapter 11: Cutting The Cord 110

Chapter 12: Management Of Debt 121

Conclusion 183

Introduction

The chapters will cover all the fundamentals you should be aware of when you are ready to look at a new way of life and a lifestyle that is not tied to a specific location or just one kind of job. In this kind of lifestyle, you don't have to be working an 9-to-5 job every day and have the freedom to travel the world. If that is appealing to you, the lifestyle of a digital nomad could be the ideal choice for you. This guidebook will help you learn how the concept of the digital nomad life is about, some essential steps you must do to begin your journey and also some of the benefits from this lifestyle as well.

It is our intention to examine the things that it is that being a digital nomad all about. We will be able to talk about the ways in which this lifestyle is different from the others and some of the main reasons people are drawn to this approach compared to some other alternatives. Then, we will discuss the other important aspect of this lifestyle that everybody should consider, such as the distinction between being a citizen of your own as well as a global one and the ways to change your status to the latter in order to help make the digital life a small bit more manageable.

It is now time to look for some of the top destinations to live the digital nomad life. It is possible to technically travel around and select any spot anywhere in the world you'd like to. We'll divide it into ten destinations that provide a lot of flexibility, plenty of activities and an affordable cost of living, so that you can enjoy like this without the hassle. While we're there we will explore what a second passport about and how to obtain one to ensure you are secure and make travel between locations that is typical for digital nomads, more simple.

The next topic we'll be talking about will be about your tax obligations. As an online nomad it is necessary to think about tax obligations and the best way to get it completed. We'll explore the fundamentals of planning your taxes when away from your home country as well as dive into the tax-free residence program , and the ways you can utilize this to save tax dollars. Living the digital nomad lifestyle isn't easy and you'll need to be able to live within your budget. The ability to reduce taxes can be a big help for you.

In order to conclude this guidebook it is important to examine at other subjects which can make becoming digital nomads simpler. We'll look at the different offshore financial institutions you might have to collaborate with while traveling and how you can make use of them to ensure that the money you earn secure and safe. We can conclude this with a discussion of ways to use offshore businesses to expand your business and experience amazing successes.

Many youngsters are excited about traveling and becoming digital nomads. It gives them a great opportunity to travel the world traveling to as many destinations as they'd like, and doing varied work that they can make use of later to establish an own company and be a freelancer after they return home. If you decide to do the same thing for just a few months, or for ten years, it's an enjoyable journey. If you're looking to know more about the process of becoming a digital nomad and the things the process is all about take a look this book.

There are many books about this topic that are available, thank you to you for picking this one! We have made every effort to make sure that it contains as much information as possible. Please take advantage of it!

Chapter 1: What Is It Mean To Be A Digital Nomad

The world changes around us at the speed of light. It is essential to be aware of the evolving nature of jobs we are able to employ, as well as how we do our work. There are many people who are moving away from the traditional workplace and working on their own at locations that are self-contained and let them enjoy a bit of freedom and not worry about the work they do. As a result of these shifts we are witnessing the beginning of something that is called"the digital nomad.

What is What is Digital Nomad?

Before we move on in this discussion it is important to examine the definition of what a digital nomad all about. They are people who do not have a fixed location and utilize the different types of technology available to complete their work. These workers work remotely, which means they can work from home to complete their work and not need to be physically present in the office.

The great thing about this is that living the life of the digital nomad is made possible by a variety of the innovations we have to take advantage of in the contemporary world. This includes tools for managing content and internet access that is affordable and accessible via Wi-Fi, the fantastic use of smartphones to get work accomplished, and perhaps even certain VoIP services which can help to finish your work and stay in touch with your employers and clients at once.

There are digital nomads across the globe. They can be found at a library in Argentina or at cafes throughout France and in office shares in Australia or even at their homes should they decide to. While this lifestyle and the idea of the idea of being an online nomad might seem attractive, it has negatives. That's why it isn't for everyone to live in this manner.

You can pick any spot you'd like and, at times, you may select a spot which is beautiful or the place you've always dreamed of but the job available may not be your best. Sometimes, they don't utilize your talents to the maximum or at other times, they won't pay you that much. Therefore, in order to ensure that you are able to maintain your life as digital nomads it is possible to be more productive and earn less money than what you can expect to earn at a traditional job.

There are numerous strategies you can employ to make your life a little more manageable. One option is to concentrate on picking the positions that offer the greatest return on your time, and discover ways to secure these contracts that will allow your earnings to rise. One other option is to discover methods to reduce costs and discover new and interesting ways to save money with accommodation sharing or homestays to save money.

The best way to ensure that you can live the new life style of becoming a digital nomad is to earn a solid stream of passive income can be used to supplement any contracts you find as you travel. This will relieve some of the financial burden to allow you to get out and explore the world and not have to be working all day.

Who are the Digital Nomad?

Although there are some exceptions digital nomads are likely to be young people who be employed in the majority of fields which fall under what is known as the "knowledge economy. This includes options such as tutoring, consulting writing and design, IT marketing, and more.

Although the majority of freelancers and telecommuters are technically considered to be digital nomads however, the term is usually being used to refer to those who live or travel outside of their home country while doing work. Certain digital nomads have diverse client base and aren't afraid to make a living from more than one work at the same time. There are also those who may have formal and even formal contracts with clients that aid them in getting an assurance of how much work perform or the number of hours they will charge in order to facilitate the process.

In time, however the digital nomads eventually be confined to their homes offices. Once they're done traveling the globe and building their client portfolios, the portfolios they build up can often help them to change from being a digital nomads to an full-time freelancer. This is possible to be able to do it from any place that they want to.

In the event that the virtual nomad has the time to think of an effective strategy for their place of residence, they can benefit from the currency and cost of living variations to locate an area where the money they earn online can be used for more and can cut down on the amount they'll actually have to put into. While some countries are more expensive and thought to be developed, digital nomads who turn freelancers typically get more favorable tax treatment than regular employees, making it simpler to keep more of the money they earn without the need to reside in a place they do not want to live.

It is possible for anyone to become an internet-connected nomad if they want to. It's typically more convenient as we get older or perhaps just out of college. We can take advantage of it as a way to gain experiences and gain knowledge about the different civilizations and cultures that are available. But that doesn't mean others aren't able to do so too. It is essential to prepare for the lifestyle you'll be living and all it offers and be sure you're capable of living on small amounts as you travel across the globe. However, it's a good chance to learn something completely new.

The life that a digital nomad leads could be extremely interesting and enjoyment in certain instances. It is possible to travel and change from one place or from one country to another at any time you'd like. This kind of lifestyle is somewhat unpredictable as you don't know what your earnings are going to come from, and you must be cautious about costs and how you'll deal with financial challenges. However, for the majority of young people who are eager to try something completely different and get away from the routine this can be an excellent way to experience various issues and lets them explore across the globe.

Chapter 2: Becoming A Global Citizen Instead Of A Local Citizen

Another aspect we should to be aware of is the difference between being a local and being a global citizen. There are two distinct notions and opinions about the world, and determining which is right for us when we decide to live a life of digital nomadism can be crucial. A few of the factors should be considered when evaluating the two choices in citizenship include:

The Local Citizen

The local resident is typically the person we meet with the majority of people. They'll be in one location for their entire life, and usually even if they relocate, they'll remain in the same place. It's possible that they'll flit around for a in some countries, and as an alternative they may be able to move to a different country. However, their perspective to the universe is limited as they do not be able to move around and stay in many nations.

This isn't always negative however it is something is worth considering since their view of the world is likely to be based on the things we observe in our daily basis. It is possible to read about different cultures and what's happening however we do not get any insight into this as we are confined to what we can see around our home.

The identity of a lot of people is tied to the community in which they live for the majority time. If they were brought up in France and then spend the rest of their existence there, it's likely to impact their identity as well as how they see the world. They may want to learn the basics of Russian or Argentinian culture , but because they've never been to either and never had the time to visit and experience it, they will not fully comprehend how they live.

The Global Citizen

If you're planning to be digital nomads you are likely to find that you'll travel to and reside in a variety of nations. This is an excellent choice because you have an opportunity to encounter different cultures, try different things, and experience life everywhere in a brief amount of time. Your perception of the world will change considerably by doing this because you're not in one place for the duration and also explore something completely different. Your identity will be affected by different peoples and cultures, particularly when you are doing this over more time.

For a closer look in detail, especially because it's so unique and distinctive Global citizenship is likely to mean that the person's identity is capable of transcending boundaries of the political and geographical world surrounding them. Furthermore, the rights or responsibilities will come from belonging to a larger class , also the human race.

This doesn't mean the individual will abjure or disclaim their nationality or local identity, either. However, it does mean that these identities will be put in the back seat to their participation to this global society. To expand this idea further, this idea will raise questions about the current state of the world in the age of globalization. We tend to focus on what everybody else is doing instead of focusing the things we do.

In a more general sense we can see that this term is one that has a similar sense to the word cosmopolitan, and world-wide citizen. But , it could be accompanied by a number of additional and special meetings that are in the contexts we're looking for.

This isn't a condition for becoming a digital nomad but it does make huge difference in how you can go through this entire process. If you're too dependent on the country you are from or are even bound to your personal location, and do not pay attention to the happenings all surrounding you, life being a nomad on the internet can be very difficult and might not be a lot of fun for you.

Because you will be changing your citizenship as well as where you'll live every day the concept of global citizenship will be a major consideration in this case. It is important to be aware of, and perhaps be concerned about what other people are living in different regions of the world as it will influence the places you travel to and whether you'll be able find employment, or even if you will be able to make itso, you will need to determine if you'll be secure or not depending on where that you are in.

Being digital nomad doesn't mean you must leave your country of origin , or that you'll never go back to that place again. This doesn't mean you won't be concerned about the country you grew up in. If you do decide to be an online nomad, you must consider that you're more than a citizen of the world, particularly if are planning to travel around often. Making a change in your perspective and evaluating your new citizenship could make the transition a more manageable.

Chapter 3: Top Locations To Be An Digital Nomad

As a digital nomad there are many possibilities to consider in order to relocate around the world with someone else and explore. There are certain places which are better suited to this kind of lifestyle , and will allow you to explore places in the world you've never thought of. Some of them are cheaper in cost, which means you'll be able to leverage your money to get your dollars to go as far as is possible. Making the right choice and the right location will have a significant impact on the degree to which you'll be able to live this life and achieve some great outcomes.

It is possible to work wherever you'd like, and it will help you get the most outcomes. If you want to ensure that you travel the world and you are able to keep the cost of living lower so that you can make your life more comfortably If so, you should look at the locations below that can help you make this happen.

1. Chiang Mai, Thailand

It is one of the first destinations for digital nomads and is a well-known place to freelancers to live and work. It is located in northern Thailand and will enjoy an acoustic and cooler temperature than other locations in Thailand. It also features a beautiful jungle that you can appreciate.

Many digital nomads have found that living costs in this region is reasonable and it is possible to connect online when you go to co-working and cafes. The area of Nimman is among the most sought-after areas for working and live. You can discover a variety of eateries as well as accommodation options, as well as food stalls on the streets. It's a fantastic option to get your job accomplished and live in a place that is affordable and explore the world simultaneously.

2. Tbilisi, Georgia

Georgia has become an increasingly sought-after location for those who travel digitally, and the use of this technology will be successful without any hurdles to cross. The year 2015 saw Georgia implemented a law which will allow people who hail from different nations around the world to visit and stay for a full year without needing an entry visa. This is ideal for the digital nomads who want to remain in one location for a time, and then intend to move elsewhere.

Cost of life in this region of Georgia is quite affordable and you will have access to internet too. Being there for the whole year will give you plenty of time to travel around Georgia, and it is a great place to travel to other countries due to its proximity to it. Additionally, Tbilisi is a bit capital city with all the amenities that the digital nomad is going to require, and you will soon realize that the people of Tbilisi are welcoming and welcoming.

3. Canggu, Bali

If you're looking for an amazing climate and a laid-back lifestyle and stunning scenery to admire every day, this town located in Bali is the ideal location. It has the fast internet that you require in numerous co-working areas, and there is a very low price of life in the region. This is the reason why the majority of digital nomads are drawn to spending more time in these spaces.

The people living in this region are extremely welcoming to tourists who want to visit in the area, and there's not any crime in the region. Additionally, you'll find that there is an enormous importance on living healthy living, so there are plenty of things to keep you entertained along the way. You can always finish a long day at work with some relaxing at the beach. Canggu can also be a fantastic place for those who are digital nomads with many other digital nomads who live there, which will assist you in networking and make acquaintances.

4. Ho Chi Min City, Vietnam

If you'd like to to reside in a huge city and be able to enjoy some of the bustle and excitement that is evident in this, but do not want the price tag in other cities offering these amenities and amenities, then moving towards Ho Chi Min City is the best alternative.

This option will give you everything that your digital nomad lifestyle requires. There are plenty of co-working places in which you can work working. If you'd want to take an escape from the chaos that an urban area offers it is fishing village of Mui Ne, just a couple of hours away to help to change things up.

5. Barcelona, Spain

There are plenty of things to do while we are at Barcelona, Spain. One of them is that it's an area where the sun will last for throughout the year. It also has lots of wonderful Mediterranean coastlines for us to explore and that is the reason it's a popular destination when it comes to digital nomads. The city will be filled with heritage and culture that the most difficult thing to deal on is deciding the things you'd like to spend your time with first!

There's a fantastic transportation system in the city which will allow you to get wherever you need to go and, for large and having all the amenities that it has, the cost of living is affordable. It also has a huge digital nomad community which means you'll soon feel comfortable. There's even a version that is similar to Silicon Valley in this city that lets you find many of the networking opportunities you're seeking. English is widely spoken in the city, and it's simple to get out and meet people also.

6. Taipei, Taiwan

If you're looking to enjoy a mix of warm people, speedy internet, delicious food and a rich cultural diversity and food, then this is the best option to choose. Public transportation is cheap and reliable. You are able to travel throughout the city, starting from the coworking hub at a reasonable price to the top restaurants in the city.

It is also easy to be able to stay for a while and then have a blast exploring. The majority of tourists that originate from countries that are developing are able to obtain a visa valid for three months once they arrive. This gives you enough time to complete the tasks you have to complete, with having fun in Taiwan.

7. Buenos Aires, Argentina

Argentina is an ideal destination to visit if you're looking to become an online nomad. It offers one of the most beautiful weather throughout the year and the stunning landscapes will make you yearn for more. With all these wonderful attributes, Buenos Aires has become an ideal destination for freelancers to go to for a chance to enjoy this type of lifestyle.

It is a city that is metropolitan with several districts to choose from, making sure that you can discover a housing type that is suitable for your requirements. Also, there is an affordable cost of living which means that your money can be used more and there are excellent options for connecting to the internet at the workstations you choose to work in. If you're looking to kick back and relax The town offers numerous choices for nightlife and tourist attractions, so you're guaranteed to be busy. Beaches are within walking distance and you'll be able to enjoy the beach whenever you'd like.

8. Playa del Carmon, Mexico

It's a real dream for those who want to become an online nomad and reap all the advantages of this type of lifestyle all in one location. It is home to a many co-working hubs, coffee shops, as well as many locations to connect on the internet. Being just a few steps distance from the most beautiful beaches on the planet It won't take long to realize that this is an excellent alternative for those who want to live a life of digital nomadism.

Living costs are affordable when you live in this region and the people are more relaxed and welcoming compared to the alternatives that you can pick. You can take your breaks relaxing or swimming and end the night with the most upscale stores, featuring the freshest ingredients available throughout the day.

9. Prague, Czech Republic

While we're there we should take the time to look at Prague which is the capital in the Czech Republic. This city is gaining a lot of recognition for digital nomads. If you compare it to some others capital cities across Europe It has a price per capita that's much more affordable than other cities. Its internet service is fast and reliable and you can also spend an afternoon in local coffee shops while getting the job completed. Additionally, another benefit for living in the city is the fact that it is to the other countries located in Europe.

Because this country is within central Europe. This makes it easy to move between countries and also there are many transportation links that facilitate this and allow you to travel from one area to another and get the most of your travels. The city also enjoys excellent weather. For the majority of the year, it is pleasant and sunny which means you'll have plenty of time to go out and experience what the world offers.

10. Ko Lanta, Thailand

The last option we are going to sit down to explore is slightly different from the alternatives available and is suitable for people who are looking to take on things in a different way. There are many digital nomads who are seeking to swap off the stress and cost of living in major cities to live a more island life , surrounded by the tranquil nature and gentle breezes. One of the places where it is possible to achieve this can be Ko Lanta, an island located in Thailand that is an excellent location to spend time living and working.

Digital nomads will be able to see that living costs is low and you'll be able to get any of the speedy internet you require. There are plenty of excellent places to work on the island. The beaches are beautiful and the weather is all year round and you'll be at ease while you get through your job effortlessly.

There are plenty of amazing places to become a digital nomad and the options are limitless and should be determined by the goals you want to achieve and the things you love the most. It is possible to choose anyplace within the world, however you should be aware of the costs for living there, as well as the amenities and amenities the country or town provides as well as other. Additionally, you'll be moving about and experience several places when you're an online nomad, having a plan is a great idea to take into consideration too.

Chapter 4: Obtaining A Second Passport

Being a digital nomad you'll have to spend many days of travel and exploring all over the globe. This is a major attraction of being digital nomad. Every couple of months, you are able to explore and experience life in various areas. It's an exciting life that you will love and have the opportunity to explore numerous alternatives and explore the diverse landscapes and other landscapes that can be found all over the world.

One thing you need to think about is obtaining another passport. This means that you'll become dual citizens and will be able to keep your nationality, however, you will be able to be a citizen of another country too. This is a fantastic method to acquire an additional passport, and to broaden your financial options as well as your options for living.

If you are planning to live a digital nomadic life style, and plan to stay in it for couple of months or even longer, the second passport is an excellent alternative to consider. Being able to have dual citizenship, or even considering multi-nationality option is an excellent option to consider when you are ready to make your life more international. This allows you to move between countries

comfort and assure that there's no government that can "own" your.

Why should I get an additional passport?

It's time to review of some reasons why obtaining this second passport will be crucial for you. Along with many other advantages, an additional passport can allow you to work and stay in, travel, bank or even make investments in locations that aren't feasible through other means. The more options you have, the greater opportunities and freedoms.

If you get the second passport, you will be able to get access within a matter of minutes to the possibility of internationalization when it comes to your earnings and assets such as those that are considered not be accessible to certain citizens from other countries. This will be the case for Americans who are often not treated well when trying to open an account in a foreign country and, in most cases, are told to close their accounts that they have already used.

Due to all the rules that are in place, foreign banks and brokerages are taking business decisions that mean the cost they will have to pay in order to get one American customer are too expensive and they aren't able to accept them at all. Setting up a bank account in another country while you're an American isn't easy to say the least, or impossible. This is not a good option if you wish to be paid and utilize the money you earn in another country while you travel.

It is also possible that the advantages that come with an additional passport will stay with you for a lifetime. You can hand down this citizenship multiple times to your children's future grandchildren, if you select.

Another possibility is to have two passports could result in greater visa-free traveling.

One advantage of a high-quality passport is the amount of visa-free travel can be done using it. Making an application for a visa must be approved prior to your trip rather than getting it at the point of entry when you arrive, can be an enormous problem. It is also a hassle to go through the hoops prior to your trip could be costly as well as time-consuming and stressful. If, for instance, you are presenting an US passport in Argentina, Chile, or Brazil and you are required to pay $160 to cover an entry fee for visas.

According to a study, Swedish and Finnish passports provide visa-free travel options to other countries. This is a great option in case you intend to travel frequently. Of course, certain countries, such as Afghanistan are likely to offer you an entry-level passport that's not very helpful. The number of travel visa-free trips that you can enjoy using your passport is crucial and should be taken into consideration while working on this.

By having a second passport you will also be able to avoid any foreign policy repercussions. If your country's government has developed an unsavory habit of stepping into the inner matters of other countries of all over the globe, this can create a huge threat if something happens and you're in the wrong location at the wrong time. Selecting a passport that has the lowest foreign policy blowback risk is a great option. As an American passport holder, you are likely to experience lots of blowbacks however, it is safer to use an Swiss passport.

An additional passport will be helpful when a government determines they require more soldiers in case of the war, or if there are any restrictions on passports or other restrictions that are put into the place. Whatever the case it is possible to keep the government from trying to place your under house-arrest, by either removing and revoking the validity of your passport at any time it wants to.

One good example could be one of the most prominent examples is Syrian government. It was in the past that it refused to renew passports of Syrians who were living abroad and suspected were linked to the opposition. This isn't a surprise and is something that was predicted by others to occur. Any kind of government could and act in the same way in that they could remove passports and citizens at anytime they want and without notice.

A second passport ensures you have the rights, and you are able to move about and travel wherever you'd want without having the government the final say on the way this works.

Another advantage is that a second passport can ensure that you do not have to live as an asylum seeker. The passport of your loved ones can ensure that you have a second base of operations and another spot that you are legally entitled to the right to live and work at any time you'd like. If the worst happens having a second passport ensures that even if it is necessary to leave your country in a hurry, you'll be able to travel and will be welcomed.

A passport or citizenship in a different country can provide you with legal rights which will ensure your protection. You'll be able to travel to the country and live and work there with no difficulties, even if need to leave at any time.

Finally, this second passport will allow you to pursue the possibility of a renunciation should you decide to decide to do so. If you decide to withdraw your citizenship at any time it is necessary to obtain another passport in order to do this. This will allow you to gain all the legal and tax benefits in the event that your first country is able to introduce an abundance of oppressive and unavoidable tax laws that you do not wish to follow.

A thing to keep in mind is that if you decide to surrender you US nationality, then the nation will charge an exit tax to people who decide to renounce citizenship and fulfill certain requirements. This puts an immense value on renunciating before you are eligible to be subject to the tax due upon exit. It's a great option for entrepreneurs and international-minded young people who have a significant portion of potential earnings before them for the near future.

One thing we must end this discussion with is that there aren't any methods to get a legal second passport that is affordable quick, simple, and easy simultaneously. It's not meant to reduce the necessity of having one. It's an excellent option to protect yourself and ensure that you're protected regardless of what happens in your home country or the the world. It will however have a significant impact on how you approach the procedure. Be aware that this process can cost you money and generally takes a while to finish.

Be cautious about the scams that are out there. It could be a huge source for fraudsters, and, in the worst scenario, it could make you less than what you began with. If you are not careful you could end up in serious problems if you have a passport that is not authentic. There is a chance that there is a wealth of incorrect advice and misleading information concerning these fake passports and they can restrict your options and create several issues. Locating a trustworthy source with whom you are able to trust as well as being cautious while conducting the necessary research to ensure the best outcomes from this.

The Best Countries to get A Second Passport

There are some countries that will be much simpler to obtain passports for and therefore the ideal area to work with if you're not sure how to get your second passport as swiftly as you can. The countries that are relatively easy to obtain an additional passport via naturalization include:

1. St. Kit

T

Nevis and Nevis

This is a great place to start with, and it can assist us take charge and achieve some great results from our passports. The country has an initiative to make citizens citizens that provide clients with an additional passport via two major programs. There's two main programs: the Sugar

Industry Diversification Foundation and the Citizenship by Investment Program, and you are able to choose which you like most.

The passport through investment is an investment program in the United States that began in 1984 and is one of the most effective second citizenship programs available.

There is a possibility to collaborate together with Sugar Diversification Foundation as well to gain access. This is a project that was launched by the government for an international tax-free haven in order to aid those who direct affected by shutting up of sugar production. The funds generated from this program will be used to offer alternative work opportunities. When you apply for this program, you'll undergo a due diligence inspection conducted on you. the cost of that is set at $7500 to the primary application, and if you're adding children on the application, it's $4000 per child. In addition, there are the other fees and charges you need to make throughout the process. One person pays $250,000, while four applicants that include you, your spouse and two children below 18 years old will cost $300,000. To raise this to six, you'll pay $450,000.

If you are interested in participating in the citizen by investment program, then you must make an investment in real estate the tax haven offshore of the country. The amount you invest must be at least $400000. The government will inform you which investments are available to use, along with certain fees that will help to complete all of the other tasks completed too.

2. Antigua

It's also possible to think about purchasing a passport from Antigua. This passport offers an investment-based citizenship program that is a partnership in conjunction with Antigua as well as Barbuda. It will permit visa-free travel to over 150 countries, which includes those from The UK, Hong Kong, and many more. There are several choices to utilize to achieve this also. You can make a $100k investment in the Antigua National Development Fund, which is most likely the easiest option to use. You could also put in $1.5 million to start your company there, or $400,000 in a commercial real property project that is government is able to approve.

This option of donation is among the most used, particularly for families. There are some tax and costs to pay for this option, but it's still a good option that's cost-effective. The applicants must be with no criminal convictions and be healthy and fit. It is not necessary to go through an interview to apply to be eligible for the program, and you don't need to travel to the country to complete the application. However, you must stay in Antigua for 5 days or more during your first 5 years, while conserving the investment and the investment, but it's not difficult to fill out.

Additionally, you are able to let dependents and children up to 28 years old be included as well as dependent parents older than to 58. There is no tax on their worldwide income, meaning you are able to move and work with no need to pay back Antigua to keep your passport. There are obligation to do due diligence and professional and government charges to think about, but they aren't as costly as other countries.

3. St. Lucia

Another option we could select is St. Lucia. It is generally considered to be one of the top investments. Bonds can be purchased through the government instead of investing in real property. It is possible to purchase around $500,000 worth of bonds and typically, the money is paid in five years. It's simple and doesn't suffer from the hassles when starting a new company as well as working within the real estate industry could be like in other nations, and you don't need to sell the bonds to receive the cash back in time.

The cost is much smaller than other locations are able to offer, making it perfect for those looking to get in. It's less than half the amount that some countries across the border, such as Bulgaria requires. You could put that money to St. Lucia and get your passport immediately.

A few people enjoy applying for a passport here because it's private and private, and no person is required to be aware that you're doing this. It is easier to get the necessary documents required to travel across the globe and it's pretty simple. St. Lucia wants people to join their country and also have a second passport, which means it doesn't have the same ferocity as it happens with other nations.

4. Panama

Panama is a good candidate for a visa program, which is called the Panama's Friendly Nations. It is a great choice to consider because Panama is a great place for citizens of forty other countries to be granted residency in the event that they have $5000 available in the bank in Panama and a second economic connection with the country. This could be something as simple as ownership of an Panamanian company.

If you're legally a resident of Panama it is possible to obtain citizenship within five years or less, if everything goes as smoothly as we'd like to believe.

5. Canada

Another option to look into could be working in conjunction with Canada. It has the ability to speed up the process for naturalization too. In the past, Canada went through and eliminated it's Immigrant Investor Program. This means you'll require work before even considering moving to Canada.

After you've been granted legal residence, you can apply to become an American citizen in only four years. It is crucial to remember that you have to complete at least a few months of the four years to be citizens. This is a requirement that immigration officials will enforce quite strictly.

You can now easily obtain another passport anywhere you'd like to go anywhere in the world. You're not restricted to only the five options which we mentioned above. The five listed above are frequently regarded as the most straightforward. It is important to conduct some study to determine which areas you'd like spend most in your digital travels and which passport is most likely to offer the most benefits in the long run. After you've completed this, you are now able to follow the appropriate steps to obtain your passport, and then use it to let yourself be more free.

Chapter 5: Essentials In Offshore Tax Planning

The next issue we must look into is how you will deal with taxes while you're an online nomad. In some instances it is necessary for tax payment to the own home country as well as the one in which you spent the majority of the time in that year. If you traveled across several countries over the period of the year it's possible that you'll need to pay taxes to all of them in addition. This can make tax planning challenging to handle, so we must discuss the options available and how you can handle everything.

When you go through this process it is possible to discover that tax planning offshore is a common practice which is not recognized as a whole because it creates images of tax fraud. However, this isn't the case so long as you follow the correct steps for doing it. This image has been released because some people had a bad reputation and set up accounts offshore with the intention of either not reporting or even misreporting the earnings and income they earned in the eyes of the IRS.

While this was a widespread practice for a long period of time, you will see a significant increase in international collaboration and enforcement of tax laws. If you intend to take part in this type plan for tax preparation, which is crucial to do so if you intend to travel quite a lot, and require to do, it is essential to be in complete knowledge of the laws governing what constitutes legal tax planning and what could be considered tax evasion that is criminal.

Offshore Tax Centers

The first step is to investigate the variety of offshore companies which are willing to compete with your business based on the fact that they can reduce the amount of taxes you must pay. They are located all over the world , and it should be simple to locate one which will benefit you regardless of the location you choose to live your online life.

You may choose to run an insurance company from Bermuda should you want to and benefit from some of the regulations for insurance companies which exist. This isn't actually illegal. It's only illegal when you set out to set the company in Delaware to lower the tax liability you face for your business in California. It is only necessary to keep in mind that you must declare your earnings and pay the tax on that. If you fail to follow through the process, you could be held responsible as a result, and ignorance isn't an excuse for tax evasion or fraud.

Tax Minimization

In the next step, we must to ensure that we reduce the amount of taxes we pay every day. If you have in a nomadic life like this one, you will not want to make it every month only to have to wait until the next only to have that a large portion of your income go to tax. However, we must make sure we're living in a manner that is local.

Tax minimization is a method that is totally legal and lets you reduce the tax burden that your family or business will have to be liable to pay the local, federal and state governments annually. For instance, you could consider it preferential to select one state over another in order to create your company since the tax rates for employees are lower in the state, and you don't need to pay more. This is perfectly legal. Indeed, some states will provide lower taxes to companies to encourage further development to the region to encourage them to grow.

Similar things can be accomplished globally but this can add some additional complications in the process as we move down. If you're a resident of a particular state or country, no which place you operate from it is still accountable for the payment of income tax depending on where you are from. This means that even if you are to the United States and are a legal resident regardless of which part of the world you earn your earnings it is still necessary to declare your income and pay the tax for America. United States.

Tax Evasion

You can travel around the globe and work wherever you'd like. You can earn whatever amount of money you want in other countries too. However, you must be able to report the money after you return to your home country after you have completed the tax. It is recommended to complete this each year, just like you do with your tax returns because failing to follow this procedure is likely put you in troubles. If you don't deny citizenship and complete all the necessary paperwork you must pay taxes on your earnings to the country you are from.

Tax evasion is considered to be criminal in United States. Evasion is a way of taking tax minimization, something we mentioned in the previous paragraph, which is legal if you follow the correct manner, and taking it a step further. If this occurs it is possible for an individual to not include income in their taxes in order to lessen the tax burden. For instance, you might earn $40,000 per year, however you can only have $30000 to claim, meaning you'll save the additional amount when it comes tax time.

This was a widespread practice in the tax planning offshore because there were some offshore havens that didn't think of this as an offense. They didn't go as harshly on people who did this, which meant it was more easy to go about it and perform whatever we desired. This meant that it was much easier for those to provide less information about their income and how it was earned, mostly because the country they lived in was not required to give this information or details regarding bank accounts when requested.

The world has changed, and this isn't a great choice to make for a long time. There's more international tax law and enforcement across the globe because the countries that were affected realized that they weren't getting the amount they were entitled to from taxes. Due to this, there are less havens in the world that make it simpler to avoid paying tax obligations. There is a good chance you'll be under the watch of the IRS when you try to keep money in a foreign location and do not declare it as income.

It is crucial to follow the correct procedures to file your taxes and pay the tax you require as you go through the process. This must be done in the countries you earn income as well as in your home country and. Digital lifestyles can be more difficult to manage and maintain, particularly if you travel frequently and need to be prepared for lots of paperwork and proper record-keeping to ensure that you're handling all this in a professional manner.

The good thing is that there are many businesses available, across every region of the globe and can assist you with this is accounting and taxes are not among your best strengths. It's much better to partner with them and understand how to properly file your taxes and the actions you can take to reduce your tax burden earlier, in order to ensure you to get the most efficient outcomes.

Chapter 6: What Is The Tax-Free Residence Program?

We'll come back to the other reasons why second citizenship can be an excellent option for those who want to be at liberty to travel and not worry about something that might go wrong with your passport or home country. It can be a great way to provide an international diversification of your travels, but the passport you have isn't likely to help you achieve you're hoping to get rid of your tax obligations. If this is your intention you need to rethink your plans to rethink our options.

It is legally permissible for citizens from the United States to have as many passports as they want. However, you'll still need to pay tax to the IRS in the event that you have any of these American passports. Other countries have the same rules and include Norway, Canada, the UK and Australia. Even if you decide to move out of the country, and never visit or set into the country for the next 10 years, you'll have to pay taxes.

Whatever your circumstance is, having an address in a country with a low or no tax even provides you with plenty of freedom. For instance, you might be aware that every government agency you interact with would like to know what nation you are a citizen of. If you're living in one of these countries with high tax rates, this will cause a lot of issues.

This is why it is beneficial to establish a residence in a nation that is zero-taxand will not try and take any income you earn regardless of whether it was made elsewhere. This is a option to ensure you're treated with respect when you're there. You can make a home here, and when you travel to another country and return, you don't have to worry about this country returning and claiming your earnings. This can spare you a lot of stress and cash.

There are two methods that freelancers or digital nomad could employ to ensure that they not pay tax at all based on where you live. They include:

1. Be a citizen of a nation that has zero tax rates. This means they don't impose any capital gains tax or income taxes.

2. You must become a resident of a state which will only charge income tax as well as other taxes on the earnings you earn while within their borders. ensure that you do not earn an income while within that country.

The United States is not one of these nations. You'll have to pay taxes if you're within the borders of the nation. If you do travel out of the country for work in the country, you'll still have to report your income. This could be a significant amount of money, particularly in the event that you earn money in different countries around the world. It basically means that you're being taxed two times every year. It can be difficult for someone who barely scrapes by, usually in the beginning.

The positive side is that there are handful of countries where you can obtain an extra residency without having to pay taxes. This will take away part of the process and make it more feasible to earn money as digital nomad. Some of the countries you might want to think about to benefit from this include:

1. The Bahama

The first on our list includes the Bahamas. This is a country that does not have income tax since they make their money through tourism. Residents of the area do not have to have to pay tax on income they earn regardless of where the money is earned. The cost for government applications for temporary residency there, something that you can renew every year, is just $1000. If you are planning to stay for a time in the United States it is possible to purchase up to $250000 worth of real estate to aid in getting the permanent residence you want or longer-term alternative.

2. The British Virgin Islands

The process of obtaining one of the work permits needed to enter this country can be difficult because of the processes involved, so while it might not be the best option for you but it's still not a bad option. If you're self-sufficient, which is what you must be prior to attempting to become digital nomads, then the process of getting this visa is easy. In most cases you can get it in a matter of the span of a month. It is all you need to do is give the company some bank statements to prove that you are able to live there, and after that you have to pay a surety bond of $1,000 and you're done.

3. Brunei

The country is so rich in cash that they don't require a large number of investors to migrate to this region. If you have a large enough investment, it's possible to obtain an apartment or even permanent residency in the country. This is a little more difficult, however it will provide you with the tax benefits we'd like in addition.

4. Norfolk Island

It will comprise three islands, and has a unique immigration status to go with it, even while it is tightly tied to Australia. The country doesn't have any income tax in any way and will allow residents of New Zealand and Australia to be citizens without any issues. If you're not from one of those countries, there are couple of additional hurdles you must jump through to prove that you're able to sustain yourself, and not have to depend on them in any way.

5. Turks and Caicos Islands

Another option to choose could be Turks and Caicos Islands. This is a fantastic option to get situated on an island, but the new residency program will mean that you will need to make a deposit in order to achieve the tax-free status you desire. Foreigners looking to be residents of the island and remain for the long haul must spend $300,000 to build their own home or renovating an existing property which is in need of renovation. They can also put a minimum investment of 750000 in a company that is majority owned by locals. The choice is yours.

6. Vanuatu

This is one of the topics we'd like to discuss briefly because it's one of the few tax-free nations where obtaining second citizenship is possible. This residency program is simple to use and will benefit those who make more investments in the country , too. Foreigners looking to settle in the country must invest around $89,000 for a year . They are able to renew their residency on an annual basis. If you make more investment than this, then you'll be able to be able to add more years.

Of sure, some of the costs for the government to support this residency can be a little more expensive. But when you think about the lower costs of investing associated with this residency and the intriguing property investments are available in the area, it's definitely something to think about if you're looking to take a trip to South Pacific. South Pacific and save on your tax bill.

There are other countries with lower taxes if none choices we have examined in this chapter appear appealing. There are some options, such as Costa Rica, Anguilla, and Georgia are excellent to keep the tax burden as minimal as they can be. It is possible to pay a fee in the process, but you don't be required paying as high for this option and can reduce your dollars as you progress through the procedure.

Keep in mind that, even if you choose to go through one of the tax-free or low-tax nations as your new residence however, you will still be accountable for the tax on the money you earn, if you're the United States citizen too. It isn't a method to save on taxes but it will give you a fantastic option to lower your taxes and put more money into your pockets since you're not paying tax on your earnings more than once.

Chapter 7: What To Do To Keep Your Money Safe In Offshore Banks

Even if you intend to relocate and carry out your work in multiple countries every year, it's an excellent idea to think about where you'll save your money and income. You could put it in the same account you had at home as online jobs allow you to make money to any place you'd prefer. However, this could be a problem in the case of an institution in your local area that is not familiar with working with international payments or exchanging money. There could be problems with the bank's perception that you have made fraudulent charges to your account.

It is also not a good idea to move your money around. It's risky no matter the location you decide to reside. One option you might be interested in working with one that is offshore. We'll examine some of the steps can be taken to create this bank offshore and also some of the advantages that you can reap from this process for your own requirements as well.

Benefits of Offshore Banking Benefits of Offshore Banking as a Digital Nomad

There are many reasons to think about working with offshore banking. For instance, if you have to take funds from the work of the account, what many charges and other issues are likely to be uncovered when you live located in Paris, France, and your bank account is located in California? This could create a number of problems and it's best to use an overseas bank. It is best to choose one that works in the country that you spend the most time . and will provide you with great service and that can keep your money secure.

There are numerous advantages to this kind of account if you're digital nomads, and we'll examine a few of them right now. Some of the most important advantages of banking offshore for digital nomads include:

1. Easy to work with located in that particular country. It's much easier to

collaborate with a bank which is located in the nation where you are spending your time the most. You can withdraw the money much easier. You can speak to the bank , and even one of the tellers or managers in the event that something is not working. It's just more convenient to be nearer than your banking institution.

2. Higher exchange rates: If you can transfer your money into an account that uses your local currency, then you can save lots of cash on your exchange rates. The exchange rate could be expensive in particular if you're paying in local currency, however, it must be transferred from that currency to USD in order to return to the currency in which you're. This is two different conversions to make use of the money, and could be quite costly. If the money is transferred directly into the local account it will require at the most, one conversion or maybe no, depending on the currency you choose to use for the transaction.

3. The sovereignty of the political banking system:

Many of the banks around the world, including located in countries like Singapore, Netherlands, and the Cayman Islands, aren't managed by the government. This means that you have less risk of your money being stolen or being frozen. This is a great choice when you're traveling across the globe to perform your job.

4. Superior customer service: It's much easier to receive top-quality customer service if you're located in the same region as the bank, and not than in the opposite part of the world. This can be helpful in situations where you need to ask questions and need to get things accomplished.

5. You don't have to worry about the bank flagging your movement as fraud. If you are a customer of an account with a bank located in the United States and then you want to move from one country to the next all over the world it could cause problems. It could appear as if that someone is trying to steal your money in a fraudulent way. If you have an offshore bank it is not necessary to worry since your bank is located in the

country you spend the majority of your time.

It is important to keep in mind that offshore banks aren't the best way to get tax-free and create problems in the process. They're just meant to ensure that we are able to attain greater financial freedom and enjoy our life as digital nomads just for a bit longer. Make sure you make your tax payments and keep adequate records to get some positive outcomes.

How do I open an Offshore Bank Account? Offshore Bank Account

One alternative we could opt for is to go to a branch of the bank you'd like to utilize regardless of where you decide to visit. It is possible to speak to someone personally and get answers to your questions. But it won't permit you to evaluate the alternatives, or see what branches of a particular bank are open, and may make it more difficult to deal with the bank when you aren't sure how secure the funds is.

If you've decided you think this would be the right choice for you, the next step is to create an account. It is important to do some due diligence to be sure that you are able to navigate through the entire process. You must ensure that you're not using this as an non-intentional tax evasion strategy or you could be liable to the punishment of a fine for doing this or any other techniques. You should select one that will allow you keep your cash while travelling, and possibly one that helps you get a good interest rates in addition.

The good thing is that establishing this offshore bank isn't too difficult to accomplish. But , you should be aware of the options as you work through this procedure. The five steps you can follow to open one of these accounts are as follows:

1. Develop a strategy to bank offshore and determine what objectives you want to accomplish. It doesn't have to be difficult. It is possible to set objectives of figuring one you trust, and one that allows you to travel the globe and still have access to your money. A good rate of interest to ensure

that you can still make some extra cash on the money you earn can be excellent too.

2. If you've got this plan established, you must look for a bank that would match this plan. You'll want a bank that can meet all your goals to ensure that you are satisfied with the outcomes.

3. After having a look through the banks in existence, it's the time to sign up for an account. It can be done in person or via the internet. Be sure to keep an eye before time to find out what charges you will need to pay when using the account.

4. Once the account is opened and in good condition it is now possible to deposit funds into it. It is also possible to configure it so that any cash you receive for your work can be transferred directly to the account, too.

5. If you're working on this account, it is important be sure to have all the reporting requirements. This will make tax and other alternatives simpler to manage without running into problems.

While opening an account at a bank isn't as straightforward than it used to be, the process does not require a lot of work. It's basically similar to doing some of your banking at home. Certain banks require customers to make an appointment. Then there are others that require you to visit the branch, and then meet with the manager. Certain banks will make things easy, while some are more complex when it comes to the procedure.

A few of the top offshore banks prefer to have you meet in person than have you complete the transaction online, and that's an important thing to look out for. They can talk with you and answer any questions you might have, and much more. If you are going to your bank to meet them in person, think about wearing a dress code that is appropriate, just as you would dress for an office meeting. This will give you to gain access into the bank and ensure that they feel comfortable with you. You are still able to wear sweatpants from time to time however when seeking to create a brand new bank account, particularly in a foreign country you must put on a nice outfit and dress to impress.

Where can I open an Offshore Account? Offshore Account

Another thing to take into consideration when we're in this area is how to create one of these accounts. It is best to find one.

in a completely different area in a different location

where you can keep your passports,

You have your tax residency You have your businesses and you are a resident

. If you're planning to stay for a few years or more in one particular country, or intend to make it your primary residence for the majority times, this is the best spot to find banks

for day-to-day use.

It is also important to consider the state that the bank is situated in.

even if the institution was thought to be secure and safe even though it is considered safe and secure Somalian however, it's not the best option to conduct your banking. Due to the wars that have been going on for many years, it's unlikely that you'd ever be digital nomads initially, and even less bank there.

It is often contingent on the specific circumstances of your individual. You must consider the place where your second passport is in the country, where you want to be spending your time and what's the easiest. Check out the costs and rewards of a bank, think about how long you'll remain in one location in comparison to another, and observe how accommodating they are aiding you in setting this up. It is also worth considering whether they have a good record of documents to aid you at the time the time for tax returns arrives, and you'll need to be concerned about taxes.

A bank account that is offshore is an excellent option when traveling to another country. Even if you're not concerned about taxes as well as diversifying your investments, an offshore account could aid you in having an account in the vicinity to put your funds. It can be difficult to be a banker located in the United States all the time when you are spending a long time within South America or in the South Pacific area. This can result in issues with the bank and they may not thinking you are the person using them when you are frequently moving around. Finding a bank that is tolerant of foreigners and allows you to travel to the maximum extent possible may be the answer you seek here.

Chapter 8: Should I Utilize Off Shore Companies To Grow My Company?

The great thing about being digital nomad is that you have complete freedom to choose not only where you live , but also what you want to do as well, but you also enjoy lots of freedom when it's time to get involved in the various jobs you can get. There is no longer a limit to what's available to the local areas. You can find jobs any part of the globe. If they're willing to employ freelancers or other professionals that can work from home and work remotely, you are able to join them. This is a part of the benefits of living an online nomad. It could make it more attractive.

This provides you with a lot of flexibility to pick the jobs you'd like to work with. If you are able to locate a job that is compatible with your current lifestyle of traveling and work schedule, you are able to be employed by any company you'd like. If you come across a reliable company with an offshore location Why not consider it? Be sure to get rid of that resume and polish the cover letter before sending it an application to be considered for the position.

Being employed by some offshore firms could bring us lots of advantages. In the beginning, we'll have an opportunity to broaden the possibilities in terms of working. The lifestyle we live in may be glamorous, but if you are limited to one area of the world is realizing that we are not doing enough. If we start the possibility of freelancing or other exciting jobs throughout the globe and we will find more enjoyable and exciting activities to take part in. Companies may also take advantage of the chance to collaborate with an international freelancer to boost their image as well.

The work is enjoyable and enjoyable when you do it. Every country has its own set of rules and their own method of working. It is possible that some jobs in Europe differ from everything else you could do in America or any other place. This can transform the digital nomad lifestyle transform into an exciting adventure which you could write about in the future. Explore your options and explore something completely new and discover how enjoyable it could be while earning a profit.

This will also prove be an excellent way to get ready to launch your own business , and become a freelancer after you return to your home and are completely satisfied with your digital nomad life. The more clients you bring to the portfolio and the more interesting projects you've completed the more easy this transfer will be in the future. Be open to a variety of new experiences. If you are willing to work anywhere in the world you will gain experiences that other people only dream of. This can be used for your benefit later when the time comes to relax and try things differently.

There are plenty of ways to apply for these amazing jobs. It is necessary do some work in order to achieve it. One option is to search for opportunities online. While this may not give you all the possibilities you're looking for however it's an excellent way to begin and make your name known. Make sure your resume is updated by using a few local websites for searching job openings and then apply for certain opportunities that seem appealing. You could try some job boards like Upwork and also because these companies will connect you in positions all over the globe.

A different option would be to get involved in the field of networking. When you are in one of these new nations, you'd like to take time to or before you begin meeting individuals and connecting with them as often as you can. This gives you to learn about local jobs that other people might not hear about, and which may not be advertised on the internet. This is the reason why choosing an area that has a high percentage of digital nomad and freelancing scene is a great idea. This will allow you discover people who can give you a good source of prospects and leads.

You can also work on some effort. If you're in the countryside and would like to take an hour or so in your surroundings, walk around and take a look at what's readily available. Meet with locals, meet shop owners and find out what's open for you to work with.

Finding a decent job as digital nomads can be challenging. Locating a local job for you to travel around, means it's not going to last long and you need to be mindful of how you budget your funds and what you do on a daily basis in this. You can also opt to go with a solution that lets you have regular workflows that are not dependent on where you are However, these are usually difficult to locate. You must be aware of this and consider all the options available. Don't be discouraged There are plenty of possibilities for digital nomads. You just have to think outside of the box and come up with your own ideas in order to succeed.

How to Get Your Digital Nomad Work

The last thing we should take an in-depth look at are some of the strategies you can use to ensure that you get an occupation that is compatible with the current lifestyle than the one you want to be living in. It will be more challenging than the traditional roles you would like to work in However, because you're being able to choose out jobs across the globe and you can find out about new culture, and more, you'll find that this is among the most enjoyable things you can accomplish in your life.

With this information in mind, let's explore ways to locate the perfect digital nomad job. This may take some time and creative thinking to ensure that you have the best possible results, but it could be very enjoyable to discover what's available to you. A few of the suggestions you can use to ensure that you get the ideal virtual nomad career, or jobs in certain cases that are available include:

1. You must ensure that this is the best style of living for your needs.

Before you decide to invest in this kind of lifestyle and spend many hours looking for jobs that you'd like to take on it is important to conduct the necessary research and question your self about whether you can handle these kinds of lifestyle changes. This kind of lifestyle can be very beneficial for many people and is fun. However, for many people those who are not, it's not an ideal choice for them at all. It's difficult and there's lots of moving and you might not have a permanent base to make your home. It is important to ensure you're taking the right choice for you or not.

Although it is romantic to travel all the time and get work out in a variety of fun cafés across the globe, however, if you attempt to integrate your career and the travel aspect it is possible that this is an unsuitable lifestyle. be the ideal fit for you. It is important to research and make sure that it is the right choice for you. You should also ensure that you are completely committed to this concept. You'll not have the luxury of additional things like you do at home, you'll not have an appropriate home for the job, so finding work and even your financial situation may be difficult, and that could make this a difficult task.

This isn't meant to prevent people from being in a digital nomadic lifestyle. If you're uninformed and not at the correct mindset when you embark on this journey you will find it very difficult for you to achieve the results you'd like from this. It is essential to be ready and have the proper mindset to ensure that you're able to carry this challenge and get positive results, and truly take pleasure in the process.

2. Look for jobs that give you the freedom to choose where you work.

There's nothing wrong with obtaining an employment opportunity in the area you choose to make your home during your journeys. However, this could limit the things you can accomplish. You can either stay in the same place and not leave the country, or must relocate and you will not have an employment opportunity for a while as you look for another. It can be stressful in certain situations therefore, you must think about securing the kind of job that's going give you the ability to work wherever you'd like. Perhaps you have that type of job, then you can find a local job to in the event of a need to supplement.

Some of the remote jobs permit you to work wherever you want, while others will require that you work from some specific area. If you're looking to secure to be a successful digital nomad, you must be focused on positions that allow employees to work at the convenience of any chair you want. Certain employers require their employees to reside in a specific area for reasons such as filing taxes, training or some training sessions that are in person. So spend some time reading through the qualifications listed for the job.

There are numerous benefits of working at an employer who doesn't care which country you're in. You can move between countries without having to think about switching jobs. As long as you stay up with your tasks you are able to take the time off you wish to take travel, change places, and still earn an income. It is sometimes more difficult to find than other however, it is a guarantee that you live a life of an online nomad for as long as is possible.

3. Find locations that have the correct internet connection

If you are a digital nomad, you'll need to make the time to work from home. You won't be working at an office job in a traditional office, at the very least most times, and the work you do will need to be conducted online via the Internet. If you live living in an area with no internet connection, it puts your job in danger, and that is not an excellent thing. Every part of the world will differ in how reliable their internet speed is therefore you must consider this in figuring out where you'd prefer to reside.

If you're looking for an occupation that permits you to travel the world as a digital nomad then the internet and a strong connection will be the most crucial things ever. You need to make sure that wherever you go around the world that you have a constant high-quality and stable internet service from one spot from one place to another. This will allow you get the job accomplished and will ensure that you receive a pay check in a timely manner to keep it up.

4. Consider what you're willing to sacrifice

If you're one who loves to travel and visit friends, family members, and family members frequently The digital nomad job can make it a little difficult. The job itself in general is likely be quite lonely, too. You won't go into the office and sit at the water cooler talking with other people. This could be difficult for those who are taking on this new lifestyle and wants to interact with people around them as much as they can.

However, this doesn't mean that you'll never socialize throughout the time you live this way. You are able to socialize with other professionals, meet people from the area, and so on. It is highly recommended. But your social interactions may be a little different than before, especially when you plan to change places and not remain in one spot all the time.

If you are planning to relocate from one place to another according to your desires and your job demands the need for frequent interaction with family and friends and the potential of making new acquaintances is something that could disappear. This is the perfect time to consider whether you're willing to let go of that type of social interaction to enjoy fun with this new world adventure.

5. Find companies that invest in digital employees

The last thing we can work with is looking for businesses, if we can invest in this type of work that is digital. The nomadic lifestyle is one that requires commitment from both the employer as well as the employee. It shouldn't be just one side or else we'll encounter some problems as we go. When we think of this in a different way, employers need to be as committed as the workers to the concept of working from any location and they could be annoyed that you're not working a set schedule. If you're able to look for a job with flexible jobs that you can effortlessly work from any moment and from any location you'd like It is a great option to find firms that have shown that they're committed to supporting employees who will work from any place that they choose.

Another suggestion we can add is that it's recommended to look into choosing a career that you will truly appreciate. Of course, there are times when it is necessary to search and select the right job since it will pay the bills and lets us live this lifestyle we would like to live. Sometimes, it's essential to work in a position that we really enjoy.

You'll have to be spending a lot of time looking at all the options available, and you'll be doing lots of work hoping that you'll discover that if you don't enjoy your work it becomes difficult to keep up with everything. You're looking for something you can keep up to date, and which you like. You could even pursue this in different and thrilling ways when you decide to become a digital nomad. So take a look at that before you're getting underway.

Digital nomadism is an excellent alternative to consider and offers many opportunities you can't discover elsewhere, and also with the other positions offered. This may not be the right choice for all people, but if you can find decent offshore businesses that are hiring and are willing to partner with someone who is looking to live a digital nomadic lifestyle and also. It's just a matter of time and effort in search of these businesses and the opportunities to work with you.

Chapter 9: Disconnecting From Matrix

"If living in this way means to live in a way that is eccentric then it should be admitted that there's something to be said for eccentricity."

Around the World in 80 Days Around the World in 80 Days Jules Verne

The growth of the social web and marvels of technology are truly amazing , particularly for people that are my age. In my early childhood and teens there was no Internet or any technological advancements like this. Technology is becoming a more essential aspect of our lives. In the course of your day, you have access to computers or tablets, phones and various other devices to stay in touch with family or acquaintances, for work, or to answer questions, organize our daily schedules, or provide entertainment or distraction. Your life can be captured by a smartphone - movies, photos, videos and music productivity tools, communications entertainment and maps financial and games.

It is possible to be in the cafe or at the beach and finish online tasks, review our financial records, upload and download files to as well as from the cloud. chat to others on Skype and talk to your family and friends, and conduct lots of business online thanks to the global network.

A frequent queries from those working in an workplace - "the 9-5" is how to transform into the digital nomad. Many people see pictures of remote workers on social media seated on a white sandy beach with laptops in hand earning a decent income and they wonder how they can achieve that. But remote work isn't as simple like the stereotype of sitting at the pool with a laptop doing your tanning.

It takes a lot of work to create the perfect revenue stream, to build a reputation and more determination to sustain it in a consistent manner that goes beyond the initial excitement of business idea creation. It's easy to get caught up on work and go to rather than escaping into a world of escape. This is why it's important to stay focused and disciplined on keeping your deadlines in check and staying in the right direction.

When we talk about the digital nomad lifestyle in this book this is not a life-coaching book, or discovering your passion from a spiritual point of view. This is in a real sense of practicality . What are you most passionate about? What are you able to enjoy doing and enjoyed since you were a kid? How would you go about it if were stuck on some island remainder of your life and had only one option? What would be the one most effective way to earn money and perhaps enjoy your job?

It's also not about attempting to take over the Internet and earn millions of dollars because the main benefit of digital nomadism lies in the fact that you're freeing time. Time is an essential commodity since you don't really know the length or duration of your life will be. It's as corny as it sounds it's about having no regrets "carpe diem" Take advantage of every day.

When you're in your final days it's not a good idea to be thinking back that I wish I had been in the country that I was in, and wish I had spent longer doing that. There aren't many people who would have preferred spending more time driving to work and in a cubicle doing something they do not like. Of obviously, work is important but doing nothing isn't a good idea. One needs to be able to manage goals and a concentration. This isn't about working for a mere four hours a week but rather doing 40 hours per week as you manage your own business and operate online however it's not as if it's work since the work is a passion for you and you're living the life and work balance you've always desired.

Do not be frightened to leave

You might have met a number of individuals who do not like their job. But, when we hear the tales from digital nomads it becomes clear that they don't really dislike their work. They are truly unhappy at their jobs. They're depressed. They are suffocated and trapped. In every one of us there's an urge to break free from the system by unplugging. It can be a feeling of being rebellious and a wanderer. Doing what others advise you to do. You don't need to be doing the 9-5 job and you don't need to put on a tie or blazer, do not have to work in a cubicle. You do not have to take an income pension at old enough and you can explore because adventure without risk isn't possible. These are just a few ways that digital nomads feel confident prior to taking the take the leap. The need to make significant changes in their lives drives them to a nomadic lifestyle.

They want freedom, which encourages them to take on whatever it takes to be successful. It's the desire or excitement that makes them want to put all their effort into. If you don't have that motivation or motivation, you might not be able to prepare yourself effectively. The need to abandon the old lifestyle behind will motivate you through the difficulties you'll face when you become digital nomad.

One of the most crucial questions to ask prior to you sell everything, leave your job, and board on the next plane to Asia is the abstinence. Are you running off or are you using it to achieve "self-development"? The old saying holds true "The grass is always greener. If you're sitting working in an office today it's likely that you're looking at the outside and dreaming of a trip in Thailand, Dubai, or Brazil to work. But, there may be many times when you're digital nomads, when you fantasize about your home, family and friends, going out to the bar, or doing your usual routine.

Prepare yourself for the Nomadic Lifestyle

If you're planning to leave your normal 9-5 job and start packing your things, you'll need be sure you're able to do this and are prepared. When you're dreaming about it your way through the night, the nomadic lifestyle is the best for you. It's full of rainbows, sunshine, and unicorns. But, keep in mind that a lot of digital nomads will eventually suffer from an element of loneliness or exhaustion from their nomadic life. Digital nomads have an approach to living that is different from other lifestyles. However, it's not the answer to all your problems.

There will be some amazing moments, but you'll also have some unpleasant ones. It's all an integral part of the online nomad experience.

In the beginning, you should not think about traveling to a variety of nations in a brief amount of time. A lot of digital nomads begin by establishing the base in a place which is affordable, and then stay there for a couple of months or longer. If you don't have a large amount of cash in your bank it is necessary to adapt your budget and lifestyle to the new style of living.

Are you considering building your own company? It will require significant amounts of money in order to accomplish that correctly. This is especially true in the event that you'd like to have more time for yourself in the near future. Digital nomads who are just starting out usually stay in hostels and Airbnbs instead of renting luxurious hotels on arrival to stay in a tight budget and save money.

Try out the 4-Hour Work Week

"The 4-Hour Work Week by Tim Ferries has sold more than 1.3 million copies and it has been translated into over thirty languages. It's additionally been named the New York Times best-seller for more than four years. The primary idea of this book is that you make you work less and earn more money as if you were working smarter, not harder. It's a great place to start your Digital Nomad journey. The author outlines the necessity to plan your time well rather than cramming everything in your schedule in order to achieve more and boost the motivation of your team.

Why not move to a place in the world that's more affordable to live in, and has a more pleasant climate? Bring your laptop and work from anywhere you'd like. This is the essence for the four-hour Work Week. The entire concept of the four-hour workweek demonstrates the fact that everyone has enough time. It is just that we don't know how to manage it in a way that is efficient. In short, there's nothing that can be described in the sense of "too much or too much time" and "too full of work."

Pursue your passion

How many people are employed in regular jobs that they actually like? Many people dread Monday mornings and wake up to the alarm alarm. Between 35 and 40 hours each week, bouncing from one paycheck to the other in many countries is now the standard. Tim Ferris recommends breaking that routine. He suggests that you take a deep look at yourself and be a part of your entrepreneurial spirit. Take a moment to think about your interests in your daily life. Find your passion, and follow it. This tip can be helpful to those who want to break free from the chains of corporate slavery and start their own business.

Apply the 80/20 principle.

Tim Ferris also recommends finding 20% of the work that contributes eighty percent of your output and leaves the remainder. In a nutshell, eighty percent of the revenue of your business is derived from 20% of your customers. This is the thing you should identify and pay attention to.

Automate and delegate your work

Ferris has also provided reasons to automate something that is able to be eliminated. He also advised against delegating things that can be simplified or automated. Another tip of the four-hour Work Week teaches you is to start outsourcing your work. If you have a job that someone else can do for you, don't wait longer to delegate the task immediately.

Make a list of things to do and not-to-do list.

It is common to create a task list, and then outline the things we must do. But, the list may contain items which don't require your attention for the majority of the time. The idea of delegating works perfectly here. Make a list of all the things you are able to delegate to someone other than you, in order to divert your focus to more important tasks for the day or coming week.

Assess Yourself

The purpose of disconnecting from the Matrix will aid you in determining if this lifestyle is appropriate for you. It will let you know whether you are digital nomads or whether it's the right time to look for an opportunity to get a new job. Do a test of being digital nomads for a couple of weeks and observe what you experience. Would you like to do this in the future? Are there things you wished you were more prepared for? Did you ever feel that it wasn't for you?

Be aware that trial runs don't always provide the exact picture of what the actual experience is like. There will be some incredible moments and life experiences that you can't get in just two weeks. However, there are unexpected and often troubling challenges that can occur in long-term time frames as well.

Chapter 10: Adventure Or Escapism

"He was controlled by the force of life, by the tidal waves of being"

Jack London

The change from a full-time occupation to one that is digital job that is location-independent is thrilling. But, like any other lifestyle change it is important to plan and make the necessary changes to avoid anxiety and to avoid feeling overwhelmed.

Some people find that changing the way they are, but some find the process more difficult and difficult.

The unimaginable lightness of being

How do we view life? An important philosophical question that lies that lies at the core of digital nomadism. Perhaps an issue that is raised in the late night. Do digital nomads need to consider life a serious matter or not?

Do we view our digital nomad existence as light or heavy? Is it appropriate for a digital nomad to consider life to be too serious (the light) and enjoy the benefits a remote life offers, and ignore all other higher-level philosophy and the burden of responsibility? This is the issue that is posed by Milan Kundera at the heart of his novel "The Unbearable Lightness of Being" and is a part of Nietzsche's notion of "eternal repeatability." The title comes from the conflict of gravitas and lightness.

The idea of lightness is of living a life in which, nothing is really important, everything is in transit and the importance is due to the fact that we're all going to end up dying. Also, what really matters is nothing is it true? Or does everything matter?

"The most heavy of burdens is also a representation of life's greatest fulfillment. The greater the weight and the closer our lives become to ground, the more authentic and true they are. The absence of any burden causes man to feel less heavy than air. It allows him to rise to heights, leave of the earth and earthly existence, and to become only half-real, his actions as liberated as they seem. Which one should we then choose? Lightness or weight?"

Milan Kundera, The Unbearable Lightness of Being

Are you free as an sailor in the high seas, or do you take your boat to the harbor to dock it and walk around on dry ground. The lifestyle of a digital nomad is attractive since you have plenty of time to yourself. You can travel and enjoy adventures while making money.

Do we wish to leave our impression on the world and not "gentle into the good night" as it is written in the poem written by Dylan Thomas? There is no definitive answer to this profound philosophical question because it's an individual choice and the reason behind the start of this path towards an entirely new way of life.

Another classic book to read while considering your future as nomads could be "How I Found Freedom in an Unfree world" from Harry Browne, first published in 1973. The text outlines the notion that happiness is the most important achievable goal in this life. The freedom to live your life in the way you see appropriate - like the digital nomadic lifestyle. Freedom and happiness are possible and it's never to be too late to transform your life.

The journey to a new Lifestyle

A digital nomad who is aspiring to become one does not rise and go on the plane without having a strategy. It is rare for this kind of spontaneity to happen, as there are many factors during the journey. Similar to your daily routine not planning your life for your digital lifestyle puts you at risk of the possibility of failure. While traveling, you can see a lot of people who are fleeing from their country of origin because they aren't happy with it or because something happened during their lifetime. In essence, they're seeking a way out of some thing and hoping to achieve happiness by living an hedonistic way of life. They decide to move to a different place and take everything they have and off they take off. Most nomads feel a sense of guilt, and are dependent on their own discipline and determination to work, because they have less work hours and living in a more conducive setting.

Absolutely, when they travel individuals will come back more open-minded, and with fresh experiences that they can bring back to their lives, their jobs as well as their health appearance, their abilities or their relationships. Traveling positively has impacted their lives.

Although the 4-hour workweek and the digital nomad model suggest that you are sitting in a hammock working for four hours per day however, the reality is that you're likely carry your issues with your. If you're depressed, anxious and discontent in your country of origin, these issues will come up in the new area. But, if you're content and happy, adept in your self-control and routines and have excellent social skills, then you'll be able to take those traits with you. Accept the fact that you are the common factor everywhere you travel.

Before you set out you need to understand the time and how you will arrive there. This implies that you have plans to accomplish at the final. Be aware of the little details since the key to the final outcome.

Eliminate unnecessary expenditures

In the end, ensure that you've taken care of your health insurance and medical. If you want to realize your dream that you can be a nomad on the internet you need to cut down on expenses since you'll require savings for any financial or emergency requirements while traveling.

It is important to cut out unneeded budgets, such as membership fees or gym memberships. Also, you can offer the items you don't use in your garage to avoid having to spend money on storage expenses. If you can sort these essential needs, your life being a nomad on the internet will take the real-life route by adopting an element of minimalistism.

Accept your new lifestyle

There are times where you are unsure about your decision to end your job or career you've been working for all of your life, but remember it's a new beginning. It's likely that you have an occupation or are doing something currently that's moving along and taking care of the expenses. It may be boring, at the office or in a grocery store. However it is possible to create an online business during the evenings and on weekends. It's a small-scale online business, a tiny niche, that eventually allows you to quit your main job.

It is possible to get an opportunity to work again in the future in the event that things don't take off. However, first, you must accept the changes and give your new lifestyle all you have. It could take some time for businesses to establish and move around or living remotely might come with inherent difficulties similar to any other kind of life style.

It's likely you'll consider becoming a digital nomad since you enjoy all the aspects of the lifestyle, like flexibility and freedom. So, don't allow these challenges to overwhelm you.

With a few adjustments and preparations, you'll be able to transition easily from a full-time job becoming an online nomad.

Another crucial aspect is to become familiar in the local language that you use when communicating with other people. Knowing the dialect spoken by locals helps you understand the local culture easier.

Select where you would like to travel in the near future and then plan it

Beyond finances, take into consideration your business's or work needs when choosing a location. Are you a creative professional? You might want to work in places which facilitate this type of work. Perhaps you would like to work in a location together with other digital nomads, like co-working spaces.

When looking for a job on the internet the best approach is to search for the right niche. Be aware that you don't need to reach out to everyone anywhere on earth You only need to reach a tiny percentage of people who are on the Internet. This means you can find an area of interest according to what you're proficient in, be it graphics or coding, design or fitness, accountancy and law, or teaching. Most likely, you'll have the skills you learned in your early years or an interest or something you're naturally proficient at.

Explore all your requirements and needs from the weather to the quality of internet connectivity co-working spaces, health facilities, and more.

Each place comes with its own particular challenges, but planning ahead, and conducting some online research will help you avoid anxiety and help you make a relaxed transition into a new life.

Consider co-working spaces in order to make sure you have an effortless change from your workplace environment, especially in the event that you enjoy having colleagues in the same space.

Some transitions from a workplace to living in a van or working from a coffee shop can be a challenge, but co-working space growth is the latest middle place for a lot of.

What are the best ways to find work Options as a Digital Nomad

Before you start looking for digital nomad work it is important to figure out what you can do to earn money online. This is what I mean by:

Do you prefer to work as freelancer?

* Do you want working as a remote employee?

Perhaps you'd want to start your own company?

It is important to determine the kind of remote job that you would like to do (if you are not keen to set up your own company). Like we said, maybe there is already the qualifications and experience required for your desired job, or you require help to determine what you enjoy online, online classes will assist you in understanding the requirements for doing the job.

You may be looking for remote jobs that are entry-level, where you can be taught by doing.

Make sure you are aware of what you can do to earn money online prior to beginning your journey as a digital nomad. If you don't know what you're looking for, it's more difficult to locate it. However, if you are aware of the kind of remote work you're looking for, you are in the right place to locate it.

Speak to your employer

The best place to begin to look for remote jobs is to contact your current employer. Find out if they'd accept you working remotely. If you're employed by an international company it is possible to research the possibility of opportunities across other regions. Consider these questions:

* Can all of the things you perform now be completed using a laptop or computer?

* Can all of your discussions or meeting with supervisors or team members be conducted via phone or online?

If so, talk with your employer. See if there's a way you could switch your job at work to a remote position. Sometimes, employers are willing to cooperate and allow you to find a replacement in the wake of the lockdowns that occurred during the Covid pandemic, after which the "new normal" becomes normal.

Although it may not be full-time right at the beginning, but you can start with a couple of days per week to build confidence and demonstrate that you are able to work at your home (or anywhere else). It is possible to take off for a sabbatical, or even to work on an oil rig-style rota to work on - then leave, in a month or months at a stretch.

Remote and online work

There are a variety of websites to find work online as digital nomad. It is possible to take on remote jobs and working as a freelancer or travelling around the world. Numerous online sites for remote jobs and applications like Fiverr, We Work Remotely, FlexJobs, and UpWork offer thousands of remote work jobs as the "Gig Economy" grows catering to freelancers and more work on temporary contracts. Numerous countries, including Estonia, Malta, and Croatia offer digital nomad visas, which allow you to better manage the legal requirements of working in foreign countries.

Additionally, you can network internationally to search for jobs in different countries by via Linkedin or Instagram as well as any other platforms for social networking.

Acquiring internationally recognized skills or highly sought-after qualifications in other countries may aid in making you more employable.

Networking

Networking is certainly one of the most effective ways to find jobs regardless of what kind of job. It is possible to use LinkedIn and look up your contacts. Anyone in your industry could be able to meet someone who is interesting to you.

Reach out to your colleagues, former employers or your classmates directly. If you've had a great experience at the company, they could remember your teamwork skills and experience. If you're lucky to be in their company, they might require someone who's like you. If not, they could introduce you to other people and recommend that you. It's impossible to predict what could occur But be aware that networking can lead to incredible digital nomad work.

It is possible to talk with fellow digital nomads (if you know of any) before you embark on your travels. You can also join digital nomad forums and groups through social networking sites, Reddit, and online to learn from other's experiences. There are many unique experiences you can have but it's beneficial to have a plan in place. You might find yourself working in different locations from the ones you are familiar with in terms of living, the languages that people speak, and the cultural practices.

Allow yourself time to adjust and get to know the place.

The advantage of being digital nomads is that, if you don't like the place you're in, you are able to relocate to another (unless there's another outbreak, then obviously!).

Chapter 11: Cutting The Cord

"Let us raise a toast to the animal world and escapism, clouds on our roofs and quick coffees, the unemployment benefit and libraries to absinthe, and generous landlords to music and warming bodies, and to contraceptives... and to the "good life" regardless of what it is and wherever it may be."

Hunter S. Thompson

Digital nomads travel the globe performing their online work where they can access an internet connection of decent quality and a life style that fits them for a price that is affordable. It's a great life, but the worldwide coronavirus epidemic has made it more difficult for a time.

But, with borders opening and flights resuming and the desire to become a digital nomad is alive and well. Indeed, a lot of individuals have decided to work online to meet the physical distancing guidelines. The lockdown has intensified already current trends and the dream of a digital nomad has been realized for a lot of people who believe that they can easily continue to do so within the next few years. The stereotypically sandy beach and with an affordable cost.

Digital Nomads have exploded as millions of individuals worked at home

According to a study by MBO Partners, 7.3 million Americans in the year 2019 were classified as digital nomadic. Between the year of 2019 between 2020 and 2019, that number was boosted by an astonishing forty-nine percent because of the pandemic of coronavirus. In the present, it is believed that there are 10.9 millions digital nomads in America in the United States alone (MBO Partners)

The causes behind the increase

A 'perfect storm' is the result of the rapid growth of internet usage and its associated apps, the feeling of freedom, increased salary expectations, more flexibility and the capability to work wherever in the world. In addition, the lockdown that will begin in

2020 and the instructions by employers to stay away from work. The growth of digital nomads isn't slowing down.

The co-founder of the famous website NomadList, Pieter Levels, anticipates that there will be a billion digital nomads in the world by 2035.

Researchers have also observed that women are the leaders in the digital age and the greater flexibility that is offered has been a boon to many women who are looking to have a baby. Before, being a mother has been a huge obstacle for women looking to pursue their career. The raising of children and the breaks from work can result in less promotions, which contributes to the gender pay gap.

But, the transition to the digital nomad altered the way of life. The freedom from the desk at work and the 9-5 routine females and other working moms have thrived in this new environment and have a way to combine work and their family lives. Around thirty percent of remote businesses have female founders, presidents or CEOs.

This is in contrast to 5.2 per cent of female CEOs working in the average workplace. Given these figures there is no reason to be surprised that women choose a nomad lifestyle.

Remote Workers are scattered around the Globe

The digital nomad trend in 2021 show that the population of nomads is very diverse in terms of nationality , and hails from all over the world. In this American population, 77% of digital nomads have white. 14 percent of them are African American, seven percent are Asian and seven percent are Hispanic and two percent belong to different ethnicities.

Additionally, digital nomads are part of every age group between sixty-five and over. Contrary to popular belief research has also shown that digital nomads aren't solely freelancers. They also include teachers writers, programmers, artists CEOs, etc. The list of jobs goes on. Research has also revealed that thirty-six percentage of these digital nomads work for various companies or on multiple platforms and not only for one.

The hospitality and travel industry is another area in which people are making the plunge into the digital nomad lifestyle.

A report released in the name of Airbnb during May of 2021 showed that the amount of long-term stays has almost doubled year-over-year. The amount of Airbnb guest reviews that mention remote work has also grown by 520 percent around the world in the past year. 55% of long-term guests surveyed in 2021 said they were either studying or working in their time of stay.

Airbnb anticipates that the majority of users will not be working at home only after the lockdowns are over however, they will be looking at suburban homes away from the city as well as forest cabins, beach cottages to different environment and to be productive.

What kind of workplaces will they be like post-COVID?

The post-pandemic scenario isn't fully understood as of yet, and as of this writing, the Pandemic isn't over. Certain patterns have begun to emerge and others have become more apparent.

The concept of digital nomads was taking off prior to COVID, and Covid has proven to be the "locomotive of change'. However, more companies are now looking at the possibilities of long-term remote work , and even pondering whether it is necessary to go back to traditional office space in the first place due to the high cost of real space.

Communication changes

The worldwide spread of the coronavirus has caused an enormous shift in the way the business owners managed their teams, defended their business models using remote working, and also how professional development and education are conducted. In addition, there's been significant growth in the use of online communications apps and video conferencing platforms like Zoom or Microsoft Teams. As a result, it has become more apparent that digital nomads are as productive and connected at a distance, as they would be in a physical situation.

More remote workers will be employed.

Businesses and organizations across the globe continue to research the advantages of working remotely. These include greater team autonomy and less operational expenses This can also mean greater job satisfaction. It seems like this type of working is going to be here to stay for a long time.

Distributed teams are now viewed as to be a long-term option instead of a temporary solution. For many digital nomads it could lead to more jobs in the near future or the possibility of more flexible jobs in the present to fit the nomad lifestyle.

The importance of healthcare will increase than ever before.

With COVID-19 increasing stress on the healthcare system globally Most predictions predict that overall wellbeing security, health, and safety will be a greater matter among digital-based nomads than before.

Many travelers take out insurance or coverage abroad prior to leaving their countries of origin It is typically because of the membership of a bank or credit card that provides such insurance. But, not everyone is living a nomad lifestyle is as organised and has explored the options for health insurance.

In light of the uncertainty caused by the residual of the pandemic it is necessary to review the number of cases currently in the country, requirements for immigration for PCR tests and vaccination, as well as the nearest hospitals that are covered by their plans, as well as any additional local restrictions or mandates.

It is more expensive and more difficult.

One of the advantages of being digital nomads is that you can save money. If you're one who travels, you could enjoy significant tax advantages. For example, if reside in America and you are outside in the

United States for at least 330 of from 365 days, you could be eligible under an exemption from the Foreign Income Exclusion Tax.

It is evident that the majority of Teleworkers enjoy huge benefits by being away from the country for a longer time. Other countries have similar tax advantages too.

Yet the airlines are struggling to keep their businesses afloat as they struggle to survive, the cost of flying has increased, as schedules have become more flexible. It is likely that the aviation industry is not expected to recover for several months, or even decades after the pandemic. It is a new territory and difficult to forecast since the number of flights have increased and airports are experiencing increased travel.

Other aspects can affect the places digital nomads choose as their temporary or permanent homes. In case you're in a situation to take your luggage and leave immediately there are other options you can do to make the whole circumstance easier to manage. For instance, you could use a "taster" when organizing a trip nearer to home.

Given the current difficulties of travel abroad by air and the current economic downturn, it could be the perfect time to jump into your car and head further away from home. Additionally, when you travel domestically, you are helping local economies that have been hit by the burden of the coronavirus epidemic as well as explore some of the undiscovered treasures on the way.

The New Normal

With Covid-19 leading a major shift to remote work The digital nomad movement is poised to grow exponentially in the coming years. Companies are increasingly shedding their office space to save money as employees and employers alike are becoming more comfortable with working from home.

The trend was gaining momentum even before the outbreak, helped by the rise of co-working areas and the emergence of digital nomad-oriented companies. As borders are slowly opened and travel returns, more and more emerging markets will try at leveraging the growing movement of nomads looking for attractive, reliable, and affordable locations to work.

Chapter 12: Management Of Debt

Overview

In the perfect world, you won't have any. As we age and become more responsible, we make some rash financial decisions and eventually end up with a type of debt or other at some point. If you do not currently have debt, then that's excellent! But, you should go through this section to make sure that you will not be liable for future debts or manage it properly if you are left with no other option. A well-managed debt management strategy does not just save your money , but also the credit rating.

Common types of debtinclude credit cards as well as student loans, car mortgages, loans and various other debts. It is likely that you have were in the middle of those debts. All debts share the same fundamental characteristics. They include the principal (amount that is borrowed) and interest rate the payment schedule and the time period. It is important to be aware of all these details for any outstanding debts that are not paid.

The management of debt isn't an enjoyable subject, but it is an essential one. One of the most crucial aspects to retirement and increasing your savings over the long term is to establish a sound plan for eliminating all your debt.

The Credit Report and Scores

Most debts will end up on your credit report. Your credit report provides an account of the degree to which you are "good" an borrowers you were previously. Potential lenders consider the information they gather to determine on whether or not they will offer you a credit card or loan. Additionally, you are able to get an credit score that is a secret formula which weighs the entirety of your credit report to assign your creditworthiness the form of a score. It helps lenders assess potential applicants and determine if they should loan to anyone or not.

There are three credit scores and reports: Equifax, Transunion, and Experian. The majority of the information contained on these three reports will be approximately identical, however it's not always. Certain banks and institutions utilize just either one of or two main credit bureaus. This is not only different by firm however also between states. They also create three distinct ratings for credit. These scores are computed differently and are based solely on the information given to the specific credit bureau.

Your credit report should be checked at least one time each year to ensure that they are accurate. The lending and banking institutions are run by humans who make mistakes. These mistakes can appear in your credit reports as inaccurate or inaccurate information. It is possible to contest items that are not correct to your credit reports through your credit reporting bureaus. The US government set up http://www.annualcreditreport.com to provide you free access to your credit reports online. If there is a mistake you may also challenge the report (usually on the internet).

When you get an account on your credit, it will have various sections. It is important to review each completely to ensure all the information is accurate. It contains every one of your previous and current credit accounts, including credit cards, loans collections, tax liens banksruptcies, tax liens, as well as other pertinent details from the past 10 years. If you've never looked over your credit report in the past, take a look through each line of your report to make sure that everything is accurate. A single mistake can cause a negative impact on your credit score, and could cause you to pay a high price in terms of credit scores, interest rates or being completely denied credit!

Student Loans

A lot of people today have student loans because of the rising costs of college. The cost of tuition and other expenses have increased rapidly over the last decade and a large number of students are required to borrow just to meet their financial obligations. Fortunately, the interest on student loans is usually at the lower end of the spectrum and also, you can have plenty of time to repay them. In fact, the interest could be tax-deductible if you are eligible!

The student loans offered are (usually) secured with that of the US government. This lets lenders offer low interest rates. It also means that they will not be erased when you file for bankruptcy. They will remain owed whatever happens, and for as long as you live! They are reported on credit reports, just like other debts. Paying on time is essential! If you don't pay on time and you ever fall behind the government will eventually take away your social security benefits.

They are different in that they provide the option of deferment (temporary suspending of payment). They also provide reduced monthly payment terms and longer payback periods for those with less. These choices do not adversely impact your credit. Additionally, some student loans can be forgiven in full or partial by the government if you are teaching or participating in or in the Peace Corps.

Certain students' loan lenders offer the possibility of a lower interest rate to set up automated electronic payment. It's never a bad idea to inquire! It can also make your life more efficient financially because you don't have to manually make a payment every month. This is a win-win situation and should be taken advantage of whenever you are able to.

Credit Cards

Credit cards can be truly great or bad, based on how you manage your money. They're designed to enable people to fall into debt and have to pay high fees and interest rates. If they are used correctly they could be fantastic instruments to benefit from some of the benefits offered to cardholders.

Credit card debt can be an extremely vicious cycle. When you fail to pay off the full amount when it's due, interest will begin to rise. The standard rate is 18% per year, however it could be lower or higher based on your credit score and the bank that issued you. If you do not pay the balance in full every month, you'll be in the process of paying much more interest on the amount. The bank that issued the loan earns handsome profits from this!

If you're carrying unpaid credit card debt that you are unable to pay in the next day take immediate action to cut off the credit card. Doing away with your balance will be the initial step to get out of debt. It is moment to devise the right debt management plan to get rid of that debt! You should make sure to spend more money than what is required every month, if you can. Any extra cash you have should be put towards the payment in addition.

Mortgages

If you're the owner of a house or any other property, you probably have secured or mortgage connected to it. They're generally lower-interest loans offered by banks using the property as collateral. If you don't pay back the loan, they may take possession of it and sell it in order to pay the loan. A loan on the real estate is seen as "good" debtbecause it is an investment that appreciates.

There are numerous types of mortgages that are available. They can be complicated and hard to comprehend. To make your life easier financially, you should consider a fixed-ratemortgage with a fixed term. This means that the interest rate is never changing and it is fixed for a time frame, such as 10 15 or even 30 years. Mortgage interest is tax-deductible when you deduct it in a way that is itemized.

If you don't have a fixed-ratefixed-term fixed-rate mortgage, it is recommended to refinance. Secure the interest rate as well as the payment amounts now. This will enable you to continue financial planning once you have your home paid off prior to retirement. It also helps you save money and time in the long run, with an interest rate that is fixed and a time.

Other Debts

The term "general" refers to a large classification! Other debts include the payday loan, pawn loan, personal lines of credit personal loans that are not secured, 401(K) loans, and all other forms of owing money to another. These are all very unwise methods of borrowing. They should be the first thing in the priority list for debts to be eliminated. Make them pay off and forget that the option exists!

Each of these methods to borrow usually have extreme to very high rate of interest. Sometimes, they are higher than what the amount a credit card charges! We strongly oppose using these "alternative" methods, since they're destructive to your financial future as well as the future. They cause lots of stress on your personal bank account.

Credit Karma App

Budgeting:

Overview

Budgeting is among the most essential steps in getting financial freedom. It is essential to establish a plan for what you'll do with your money. This includes deciding how much money to allocate for savings, debt repayments and investment. As time passes your budget changes. Make sure you have a budget!

Budgets aren't an interesting subject, but they are essential to long-term financial performance. There is no way to save huge sums of money accidentally. You must be aware of where every penny is going to be spent in order to stay ahead and remain ahead. Any major changes in your life could result in an adjustment to your the budget. You should check it every month to ensure you're staying on the right track.

The process of creating a budget for the month

The first step to create an honest and realistic budget for the month is to look at your expenses over the last twelve months. Keep track of statements from your bank as well as credit card statement as well as your tax return for the prior year. You should add up every bank account withdrawal and credit card transactions, and any payments made to pay tax purposes (ignore all tax-related refunds due the moment).

When you have all of your expenses tallied then divide the sum by 12. This will give you your average monthly expense. It's a good base for your budget for the upcoming twelve months. You can include any major expenses you know that you are likely to incur since they'll need to be included in your budget. Be aware that this is strictly for personal costs and not for business expenses. Businesses are responsible for individual budgets!

Your annual income must be in line with or possibly surpass your annual expenses. The next step is to calculate your income!

The next step is to be aware of your income from the past twelve months. The best place to start is your tax return from the most recent full year. You can utilize your "adjusted total income" figure and subtract the tax that you paid. Make sure to subtract Social Security and medicare taxes, too! In the event that your earnings have fluctuated dramatically from your previous tax return, you should use your best judgment. Combine your real earnings over the past 12 months to create the number you can work with.

Find your monthly average earnings by subdividing the annual earnings by 12. This is particularly useful in the case of income that is irregular or inconsistent. Many business owners are experiencing inconsistent income. The objective is to arrive at an annual number to base your work. The actual results could be higher or lower, in most instances. We're making the best guess based on the information we have.

Now , you can calculate your monthly income figure and subtract your monthly expenses. In the worst case, it should be zero, but at a minimum it should be it should be a positive number. If it's negative, then you're likely to be in debt or will be in the near future. In every case, it is necessary to break the number into groups.

At a minimum , your costs will fall into the following categories:

* Housing

* Utilities (phone internet, phone water, etc.)

* Dining and eating

* Entertainment

* Clothing

* Transportation

* Minimum debt payments

* Healthcare

• tax (if self-employed)

Review your previous 12 months of statements for your bank and credit card statements and tax statements (if employed) to get numbers for those categories. If they're not exactly the same every month take them all together and then divide them by 12 to come up with an average amount to complete. This can require some time, but the effort is well worth it! You'll have an impressive comprehension of the money you spend.

Once you've got your costs per category it is time to prepare the initial sketch of your budget. Then, you'll want to examine each cost in each category, and identify areas where you can cut costs. The aim is to free up some of money to put towards paying off the debt or to increase savings and investment funds.

After you have adjusted your budget to reflect any new cuts and cuts, you will have more money available than you have expenses. If you're in debt, the bulk of your money will be used to pay down your debts faster. Begin with the lowest debt (total amount due) and move upwards. Be sure to pay more than minimum when feasible!

The Emergency Fund

Every person ought to have an emergency savings account. There are no exemptions. These are savings that you have put aside for unexpected costs that life can throw at you. Examples: Your laptop dies. Your car requires costly repair. You'll need to pay for an expense to a hospital. You can see the picture!

Emergency Fund Phase 1 (critical)

The ideal starting point is $1,000. It's not enough for every situation, but it's a good amount to keep in mind. If you're in debt, it is recommended to build up your emergency fund to $1,000 and then make higher than your minimum payment due. Saving this money will prevent you from adding debt in the future when something happens, and is likely to happen!

Save your emergency funds in an account for savings that is separate from your regular one. It will be simple to determine how much money you have. Incorporate money each month (even the smallest amount of five or ten dollars) to reach the goal of $1,000. Use any unexpected income to boost the amount. If you're able to get $1,000, transfer the funds to debt payments If you're in debt. If you're free of debt, then you can move to Stage 2.

Emergency Fund Stage 2 (optional however strongly advised!)

Stage 2 is intended for self-employed people, those with irregular or fluctuating incomes, and retired people. Apart from having an emergency fund of $1,000 It is recommended to have 6-12 months of your basic daily expenses in savings in your emergency account. The idea is not to be worried about cash to cover your daily expenses, or for stock market fluctuations and downs.

Self-employed people and those who earn periodic or irregular incomes may need money to help cover seasonal downturns, poor sales periods, or to transition in new endeavors. The idea of having 6-12 months of cash saved up to live on can greatly ease stress. This sum of money is a long time to accumulate but it's worthwhile when you require it. Make plans for the worst and then work towards the highest quality!

Retirees should also have six to twelve months of expenses in cash as well. This lets you take advantage of hard times in the markets as well as other financial downturns. This also eases withdrawals of cash from investments for retirement as there's no need to sell the investments each month. If you fall below 6 months' worth expenses for living, you'll have to cash out additional investments to bring it back up.

Travel Budgeting

Travel is a vital part of the digital nomad's lifestyle. Making plans for long-term (expensive) travel in the near future will allow you to adjust your budget for the month to account for it. If you are certain you will need to travel during the year ahead, ensure you include the "Travel" section to the budget for the month to fund it. An additional savings bank account specifically for travel is helpful if you anticipate a major travel purchase to happen so that you can make savings towards the expense each month.

In addition, you should include travel insurance in the budget. We will discuss the specifics on travel insurance under our insurance section. It's inexpensive and extremely important if you are in need of it. Be sure that you're protected!

Other items that are included in the travel budget include: weekends and holidays and flights that are short-haul as well as other trips you plan to take. Incorporating them into your budget is not having to draw from other savings to cover these expenses. Make plans as far in advance as you can! Calculate your expected costs for all trips you're sure to undertake. Divide that sum by 12 and place this amount into your savings on travel each month.

Mint App

Insurance:

Overview

Insurance can be complex and boring and can be costly depending on the needs of your. With the variety of insurance options, it can be difficult to determine the type of insurance you need, or where to begin. This section will cut the field down to most important and will explain each type in depth.

The most commonly used type of coverage is:

* Life

* Health

* Automotive

• Homeowner's and renter's

* Travel

At some point in your life you'll have to take advantage of the various types of insurance. Certain are fairly inexpensive, while others will consume the majority from your savings. Getting the coverage you require for the best price is essential. It is also important to make certain that you don't have too much insurance based on your financial circumstances.

Life Insurance

Life insurance is an insurance policy which pays you should you pass away during the time that it is still in effect. It's intended to pay money to your loved relatives in the event of your passing. It is crucial to obtain when there are children. It will ensure their financial security in the event of your absence. It also helps help you pay your final costs (funeral expenses, legal fees for example.).

Most people who have the need for life insurance will purchase the term insurance. It is the most basic kind of life insurance, and can meet almost all possible requirements. Term life insurance is a policy that covers your life for a specified period of time, and offers an annual payment in the event of your death. For instance, you might be a beneficiary of a 20-year life policy which pays out $250,000. If you die during the 20-year time frame, $250,000 will be paid out to the person you name as your beneficiary.

Life insurance for term is the most affordable type that you can get life insurance. You pay a monthly premium that keeps the plan in effect. Life insurance policies in other forms have a cash value, but they are also more expensive. In the majority of cases, you're better off buying term life insurance, and then saving the money you save on premiums to yourself. Life insurance is generally less expensive when you're younger. This is the perfect time to think about purchasing life insurance if you require it!

Health Insurance

Health insurance is among the most expensive forms of insurance you can get. Health costs are rising quickly, and the premiums for the health plan are likely to rise along with these costs. The United States, health insurance is a major business, with numerous kinds of insurance plans available. Every person's needs for health insurance are different and you must determine which policy best suits your personal needs best.

The most significant differences in health insurance policies stem from the amount you have to pay out of your pockets versus the amount that the insurance company must pay. The annual deductible will be the sum that you must pay prior to when the insurance company begins to pay for you. The co-pay is the amount you pay out of your pocket every time you visit the doctor, clinic or hospital. It is also the case that you have to pay co-pays for prescription drugs at pharmacies. Co-insurance is the amount you will have to pay once your deductible is met.

Examples of health insurance policies in numbers:

A Monthly Fee of $300 per month

Deductible: $2,500

Doctor visit co-pay Doctor Visit co-pay: $25

Emergency Room co-pay: $300

The Coinsurance rate is 10% or 90% after deductible has been fulfilled

Out-of-Pocket Maximum: $6,000

In the previous example 10% / 90 coinsurance is that you be required to cover 10percent of expenses above the amount of the deductible (in this instance $2,500). A policy with zero coinsurance or 100% means you will pay no more than the amount of your deductible. The maximum amount you can pay out of pocket is the amount you pay once you've paid $6,000 for uninsured medical expenses the insurance company picks all of the charges incurred thereafter for the entire year. Co-pays will always be a part of the policy regardless of the amount that you pay on most health insurance policies.

The method of calculating your coinsurance, deductible, and out-of pocket maximums is generally determined by what is known as the calendar year. If you reach all the maximums within one year , they will are reset in January 1. If you need a procedure that isn't urgent, it is better to get it only if you've already completed your coinsurance, deductible and out-of pocket maximums for the calendar year prior to the resets.

Automotive / Car Insurance

Within the United States, anyone owning and operating a motor vehicle has to be insured for their automobile by law. Each state has the ability to establish the minimum requirements for insurance, but you have to be covered regardless of which state you reside in within the United States. If you're covered by auto insurance, it will cover the cost of renting a vehicle and also.

There are two kinds of auto insurance which are: liability-only insurance as well as "full insurance."

State laws on automotive insurance differ. Also known as "no blame" states have a system in which everyone is responsible for their own damage through their own insurance. The minimum insurance requirement usually covers this. This insurance covers the property damage as well as injuries that result of an automobile accident.

"Fault" states operate an arrangement wherein one party in an auto crash is determined to be "at the fault" as the other party (and the insurance company) must pay for all injuries to the other's property and any injuries. They also have to pay to pay for any injuries they suffer as well as damaged property. The person who is at blame is typically issued an citation for traffic violations by the police following an accident.

Liability-only is the lowest cost auto insurance, and it is the type of insurance law requires you to carry. It provides the minimum amount legally required. If you own an older car that is not financed and has a low value, it is sufficient. If you are involved in an accident and you're the one to blame it is likely that you will get another vehicle or get the repairs you need to make at your own cost.

Liability-only insurance does not cover any damages or injuries to other people. If you're injured and/or damage to your car, you'll have to pay for these costs yourself in the event that you are determined to be responsible for an auto crash. Be sure to have funds to pay for this in the event that you choose to purchase only the minimum amount of insurance!

Full coverage auto insurance provides the minimum state requirements, plus comprehensive or collision coverage too. The requirement for full coverage is usually for all cars that are either leased or funded. If you're responsible for an accident, damage to your vehicle and others are protected. Collision insurance covers the event of damage directly resulting from an auto crash. Comprehensive coverage covers fire, weather and other damages that are that are not directly connected to an auto crash. Certain insurance policies provide one or both kinds of insurance based on the needs of the customer.

Full coverage insurance includes an minimum deductible ($500 is the norm, but it could be higher or lower). If your car is damaged are serious enough, your car could get declared "totaled" (a full loss that is no longer worth the expense to repair). Then, you will receive a reimbursement from the insurance company according to the value of your car. This is the case regardless of whether you were the cause of the incident or not. The deductible is only applicable to claims made against your insurance policy. It isn't deductible when another party is accountable for the damages.

It is important to look at your financial and financial requirements in order to decide the type of insurance for your vehicle is most suitable for your needs. It is possible to evaluate the costs that full coverage auto insurance with the minimum insurance required by the state. You can then decide which is the best option for your needs. Think about this the following question: If I have liability-only policy and an incident happens the next day and I'm in the wrong, will I be able to be able to pay for another car? If you can answer yes, then liability-only insurance should be able to help you. If not then you ought to think about having complete insurance.

Insurance for Renters and Homeowners.

Homeowner's insurance can be described as a type of insurance widely considered to be compulsory and inevitably. When you have a house and you have a mortgage, or other debt using the property as collateral, you'll need to carry insurance on the structure. Insurance for homeowners protects the structure as well as the property within the structure from loss. This covers fire, weather damages, structural problems and so on. In addition, it usually protects against liability in the event that someone is injured or has their property damaged within the house. Certain policies exempt certain events and therefore you should know what's included and what's not covered in your policy.

If you have a house that you rent out to tenants, you could change the coverage to "landlord insurance" that covers the house it self, but not the contents. It meets the requirements of almost any loan or debt to the house. It may be more affordable in certain cases. Be sure to have the appropriate insurance coverage even in case you do not live in the house at the moment. It also covers lost rent in the event that the property is not fully occupied due to incident caused to property. The insurance provides liability insurance.

Renter's insurance is the equivalent for landlord insurance. It protects your possessions within the home you live in as a tenant. The policy also covers responsibility in the event that someone gets injured or property is damaged in your home. If the rental property you are renting is damaged or uninhabitable it is usually protected for hotel costs as well as other expenses related to your loss of usage. Renter's insurance generally isn't expensive , and you should consider it in case you rent the property for long-term. Be sure to understand the coverage and what's not covered under your policy.

Travel Insurance

Banking:

Overview

Over the past 10 years, banking has been made a lot more simple. Banks have become more competitive to gain your business. Costs have decreased significantly for the average consumer, and the advent in the use of Internet allows you to manage your financial affairs significantly simpler. However, you have to ensure you are using the right financial option for your personal circumstance.

Be on the lookout for any fees your bank is charging. These include monthly maintenance charges, ATM fees, minimum required balances as well as other fees. If you frequently travel abroad You should also be aware of foreign exchange charges when you make transactions that involve different currencies. Banks alter their fee structure periodically and it is important to ensure that you're up-to-date on these fees.

Bank Fees

Nowadays, there's no reason to pay monthly maintenance fees or other charges just to have your account with one particular bank. Ideally, you should have an account for checking that is free of no fees for monthly maintenance and has no minimum requirements associated with it. If you're paying monthly fees on your current checking account, it's time to look elsewhere. There's almost always an option for free that's similar to, or even better than the current account!

ATM fees aren't restricted to the fees that is charged by the ATM you're currently using.

Some banks will also charge another fee in addition to the first one! If you frequent travel make sure you choose an institution that has many ATMs with no fees, or even they will pay the ATM costs. A lot of online-only banks provide this as an additional benefit when you have a bank accounts with them!

Always try to cut down on all bank fees to zero whenever feasible. They add up fast and can seriously affect your financial situation! Take the time to research local credit unions and online banks to locate the most affordable deal that meets your needs.

Foreign Transaction Fees

Foreign transaction costs are a major source of income in the world of financial institutions. They can amount to as high as three percent of the amount of the transaction! This can save you money for people who spend a lot of time in foreign countries. Be sure that your bank does not charge you for transactions made in foreign currencies!

Credit cards may also charge fees for foreign transactions that can be as high as 3 percent. If you are planning to travel abroad make sure you have the right credit card which does not charge charges for foreign transactions. The fees are generally charged regardless of whether the transaction is processed in your local currency. There are a lot of annual-fee-free credit cards that don't charge an international transaction fee.

If you're spending the majority of your time abroad , you'll probably frequently use ATMs from foreign banks. Certain ATMs charge a fee just because you're using a card from a different country. Certain financial institutions provide ATM fee reimbursements throughout the world. With an typical ATM charge of only $3. This could be a significant saving for your wallet!

Checking Accounts

The right bank account is crucial to your long-term financial security. Always be able to access a checking account that is free and does not have the bank fees mentioned above. It should be linked to an Visa or Mastercard debit card with a branded logo attached to it to allow for quick access. Online bill payment is common nowadays and lets you pay your bills online from any location. It must have access to an extensive range of ATMs that are fee-free to make cash-free access easy and.

If you often travel to foreign countries then you need to take it one step higher. Certain institutions offer international ATM cost reimbursement! This is an essential feature for anyone traveling around the world as ATM fees can mount up quickly. Also, you need to make certain that they don't add on foreign transaction fees too. Making a comparison now can save hundreds of dollars later!

Savings Accounts

Everyone requires a place to put your emergency funds of $1,000. Savings accounts with high interest rates are the best option. Online-only banks usually provide the highest interest rates on savings accounts that do not have requirements for minimums or fees for maintenance. Compare rates to find the best rate and then put your emergency funds there. You're hoping to earn interest on your cash while it's sitting!

Free savings accounts that do not require a minimum balance are ideal to achieve your goals. If you are planning a major future purchase that you're saving for, you can create savings accounts to deposit the funds each month and earn interest till the date of the purchase. Examples of goals include a replacement laptop or car, the down payment to buy a house or a trip to another country and so on.

Taxes:

Overview

Disclaimer: Every person's tax situation is unique. This is intended to be an overall guideline for handling tax-related income. It is recommended to consult with a qualified tax adviser to ensure you're following the correct procedure. Tax codes are subject to change every year. The information provided can be changed at any time.

Taxes are an inevitable part of life. There is no legal method to get around taxes. The USA has a complex tax system, with federal as well as state and local taxes to be negotiated. There are many tax codes that define which taxes are taxed and what deductions are allowed to pay taxes, and penalties for not handling your personal tax obligations correctly.

In spite of whether you owe taxes or not regardless of whether you owe any tax, you are legally obliged to submit a tax return every year. People who work full-time are able to file a straightforward tax return to complete. In the event that you are the owner of a house or own an enterprise, work as an employee or consultant and have investments or earn any other type of income, it will require more time and documents.

IRS International Earned Income Exclusion

If you are a digital nomad, there are many advantages of working and living in another country from a tax perspective. You could be eligible to be exempted from taxation on foreign earned income,, which could substantially reduce the tax burden. The exemption stipulates that you have to be out from in the United States and territories for at least 330 days during 12 months. If you are eligible, your first $100,800 in income can be exempt of federal tax. It is important to note that this exemption does not apply to self-employment tax.

States and local taxes

Tax policies for local and state governments differ widely. Based on the country you declare as your residence within the United States, you may still be required to pay state and/or local income taxes on a portion or all your earnings earned overseas. A common method is to make a decision to reside in the state that doesn't pay state income taxes. Other states could be able to take foreign earned income exclusions from the

Federal government into consideration. Make sure you consult an experienced tax professional about your particular situation.

Quarterly Tax Payments

If you're self-employed or consultant or contractor who is not covered by automatic withholding of tax then you must make quarterly tax payments to the federal government. This applies to federal as well as self-employment taxes. The majority of states that collect income tax also require quarterly tax payments to ensure that they are in compliance. The process of paying "quarterlies" can be a hassle but it has to be completed to avoid interest and penalties later on.

Form 1040ES is the form used to calculate your federal tax liability for the quarter. It lets you consider any deductions you anticipate to claim on your tax return in the end. Estimate your earnings for the year and then make installments each quarter on the due date set by IRS. The date is usually the 15th day of the month following the conclusion of every quarter (April 15th and

15th of July, as well as October 15th and the 15th of January). The exact date could be a bit different when the 15th occurs on a weekend or holiday.

The great news for those who travel digitally is that they can pay monthly tax payments online or via phone using the debit or credit card, or via phone. The IRS offers a variety of approved services that will collect taxes from you and forward these to IRS. These services all charge fees, so make sure to compare the one that costs you the lowest amount.

If you don't pay your taxes for the quarter on time and on time, you may be liable to penalties and interest on taxes that weren't paid. We strongly suggest that you speak with an experienced tax professional to ensure that you are accounting for taxes correctly and in time. This is particularly important when you're just beginning your journey being a nomad digital but don't know the procedure but. Do not pay tax extra due to a minor error!

Turbotax App

H&R Block App

Travel Hacking to The Digital Nomad:

Overview

The topic of travel hacking that has gained popularity in recent times. This is due in part to the digital nomads seeking cheap ways to travel when they work. Everyone is able to gain from doing some research to save money on travel costs! All you need is your time and experience.

Anybody who speaks of travel hacking typically refers using points and miles to pay for hotels, flights rental cars, as well as other travel-related costs. There's a vast complex world of points and miles. It's good to know that you don't need to be knowledgeable about everything to begin. Start with a good program and continue to studies while you work out which programs will be beneficial to you. You can also develop.

Miles and Points

Miles for Airline

Every airline has one type of reward or miles program that it is possible to earn points for "free" flight tickets later. It is common to use them to pay for their own flights, as in addition to any and all partners. If the airline is part of an alliance (a vast group of airlines that have a partnership with one another) it is usually possible to gain access to these flights when redeeming miles. Be aware that these flights aren't completely free, as airlines continue to charge taxes and other surcharges which are included in the flight ticket.

The purpose behind airline frequent flyer programmes is that they offer empty seats that are not intended for sale to faithful customers that have enough points earned enough to "pay" for these seats. The idea of frequent flyer programs grew as it was expanded to hundreds of different ways that customers could earn points. Today, consumers get more miles by engaging in non-flight activities, rather than actual flights. Programs for frequent travelers can be a profitable business for airlines too!

Where do you begin? We suggest you begin with an airline you fly with the most often. You can sign up for the frequent flyer programme and make sure to mention your membership number on all your bookings. Learn about the airlines they partner with so you're sure to earn more points when you travel with them. Go to their website to find out the other partners that give you miles on products and services you already have. Most people could be a deal that works with an airline based in the US. They usually offer the lowest amount of fees when you exchange miles to pay for flights.

Hotel Points

If you are a frequent guest often in chain hotels you must be a part in their loyalty program(s). For every night you stay you are rewarded with points which you can later earn free night nights. In contrast to frequent flyer programs, hotel stays you pay for in points are usually free. Simply redeem the points and pay no cost for the night. If you are a frequent guest often, you could earn elite status which grants advantages like room upgrades or free meals as well as other benefits.

Many chain hotels also provide discounts on rooms booked by members of their loyalty program. If you are being at a particular hotel or group of hotel frequently it is advisable to research discounts that are offered and how many points you need to accumulate before you can enjoy a night free that you can use. Many programs award points based upon the cost of the hotel ("X" points for every dollar you spend). If you want to redeem your points, they usually classify their hotels in a category with an established cost per night, with regards to points. This can be used to your advantage and save cash.

Travel Hacking using Credit Cards

If you're in a position where you have the option of using your credit card frequently it is possible to earn points or miles with the right credit card. If you're living and working in another country, make sure the card you purchase does not have foreign transaction charges!

Don't spend more than you are able to afford on credit cards. If you're unable to pay off the balance in full every month, we strongly suggest to avoid them completely. The costs and interest surpass the points, miles and other benefits you get.

There are a myriad of credit cards available at present. Most loyalty programs (airlines hotels, airlines etc.) offer a credit card that allows you to earn points when you spend on the card. Most of them come with individual and business versions. It allows you to earn rewards for both personal and business expenses in one loyalty scheme. Most loyalty programs offer a specific amount of miles for every dollar you spend on the card. Points are transferred to your loyalty program each month, as soon as your statement arrives (in the majority of instances).

Some credit cards include reward categories for spending. Bonus categories can offer higher rewards per dollar. For instance credit cards can give 1 point per dollar spent. Additionally, they may offer two points for every dollar for dining out. That means that if you make use of the card at the restaurant, it will award you with 2 points for every dollar you spend. Be aware that the type of any particular company is determined by the company that issued the card. Most of the time , they are right, but not always. You might find certain instances of error.

The majority of card issuers will offer an incentive to apply for the first time a card linked to the loyalty program. If you're accepted and you meet the criteria, you can be eligible for the bonus rewards offered.

Examples of Sign-Up Offers: Pay $3,000 over 3 months to get 50,000 bonus points.

In the previous example you'd earn reward of 50,000 points if can utilize the card to make $3000 worth of charges over three months. Refunds are not allowed and be deducted from the $3,000 in progress. Make sure you hit the deadline earlier to ensure you don't get disappointed in the future!

Begin with a credit card that has points on the loyalty program you'd like to join. The frequent flyer programs offered by airlines are the best ones to begin with, since the cost of flights tend to be more expensive but will require less points for redemption.

Find out what the purchase you're looking for costs and make use of the credit card sign-up bonus to get there quicker!

Cash Rewards Credit Card

Credit cards that provide cash rewards on purchases shouldn't be ignored. If you have points and miles in reserve for requirements for redemption, then you'll earn money back on your purchases. Points are a significant value in certain circumstances however, cash can buy almost anything.

There are numerous cashback-earning credit card options on the market. Some offer greater cashback for spending them for travel or other areas. Some offer the same amount regardless of what you intend to use the cashback on. Choose the one that is most effectively for your spending habits.

The most important factor to consider when choosing which card to choose is the 2% cashback. There are some cards that offer cashback of 2% everywhere, with no annual fees at the date of writing. Never accept less than 2% in rewards for a cashback credit card. If you come across a card that gives more than 2% value for redemption on a spending category that you frequent, then consider it! Be sure that you're receiving at least 2.2% per month for every purchase.

Cashback cards often offer a welcome bonus when you sign up. They generally offer smaller bonuses particularly in the case of cards that have no annual fees.

Example Sign-up Offer: Pay $1,000 over 3 months, and you'll earn $50 cashback.

The signup offer mentioned above you will get 2% cashback, plus the bonus of $50 cashback if you made a purchase of $1,000 within three months after signing up for the card. If you're looking for an additional cashback card, be sure for an opportunity to sign up for a bonus. Increase your cash earnings!

Bank-Specific Loyalty Programmes

In recent times banks have been entering the loyalty program industry by introducing its own point currencies. The value of the points currencies varies but all have the possibility of redeeming these for cash, and also transfers to loyalty plans as well! This offers the most flexibility for you and is an excellent choice for anyone who wants to use only one or two credit cards.

The USA There are 3 main bank loyalty programs that are worth looking at:

* Chase Ultimate Rewards

* CitiBank: ThankYou Points

* American Express: Membership Rewards

Each of these three programs comes with credit cards linked to these programs. The card earns points in the program by spending money with the card and by making use of services and products offered by banks' partners. You can choose the best method to redeem them cash or travel redemption, statement credit and transfer-to-partner loyalty program.

Each bank has a partnership with specific hotels and airlines which allow the transfer of your bank rewards points to reward programs for a predetermined price. Most of the time, the rate is 1:1, but it can differ slightly for certain programs. Make sure you know which bank has the most valuable points to transfer money depending on your requirements.

Every bank has a variety of credit cards for both business and personal which earn bank program points to spend on the card. It is usually possible to combine personal and business balances to consolidate your earnings in one location. They will remain flexible until they're redeemed. This is extremely beneficial, since you can choose later whether you need money or travel funds, or even the transfer of funds to your loyalty account to make the purpose of a particular redemption.

The various cards that they provide with these banks offer rewards along with bonus categories. A majority of the personal versions offer additional rewards for dining and/or travel. The business versions usually provide bonus categories for commercial purchases like office items and shipping. Make sure you choose the card with bonus categories that you frequently use. Be sure to look for bonuses when applying!

Car Insurance Coverage - Credit Card Car Insurance Guarantee

The majority of digital nomads and travelers are likely to require a rental car at some time. Certain credit cards offer the option of insurance for rental cars. Make sure you are familiar with the benefits and what's not covered by the insurance provided by the card issuer. It is usually automatic and is free when you make the rental payment to the card you are using.

The majority of rental car insurance options cover damage caused to your vehicle. Only a few offer liability coverage. You should ensure that you have the rental insurance you require within the range of what the credit card gives at no cost and what the rental business provides as a pay-per-use option. Take note of whether the insurance provided by your credit card is the only one. Certain cards offer only benefits that are greater than your insurance policy for your vehicle.

Credit Card Loss / delayed luggage coverage

Some credit cards provide protection for delayed or lost baggage on flights you purchased using the card. Airline's policies have their own rules regarding delayed or lost luggage, too. If your luggage gets delayed or lost or damaged, you may make a claim through your credit card company to receive reimbursement. This is an excellent way to aid financially in the event you have checked your bag(s) have been lost or stolen.

This is an advantage you'd like to never have however it's useful if you need it. Losing luggage can be stressful and costly so having this insurance is an excellent benefit. This coverage will reimburse you for the cost of incidentals if the luggage gets delayed, or generally a fixed amount if the luggage is lost and never returned. Make sure you make payments for flights using the card with this benefit if it is available!

Airline Cost of Baggage on Credit Card Benefit

Certain co-branded airline credit cards provide one or two checked bags when you are the card's owner. If you frequent flights and are paying for fees for checked baggage, you need to think about the possibility of a credit card that gives the benefit of free baggage allowance. Although these credit cards tend to charge an annual cost, it could be offset by savings on checked baggage when you use the benefits frequently enough. With the typical baggage cost at $25, and the average annual fees of $80, you can imagine how fast this could reduce costs!

Being "Bumped" from a flight Hacking Travel Hacking

Sometimes, flights are being sold out. The airlines attempt to determine the number of seats they will sell, and then have the plane take off full. They use secret formulas to tell the number of people who generally miss the flight or don't show in. These formulas aren't always accurate and can result in more people waiting at the gate than seats are available.

If this occurs when this happens, the agent in the airport will request for people to help take an alternative flight. It could be to one minute further to days later subject to availability. If you're willing to put in the effort it is possible to volunteer. If you do this you will be paid by the airline for the time you spent.

Compensation for the loss of you seat(s) in a plane differs. In the simplest case you will receive cash or credit towards the next flight. If you plan to stay for a long period of time or for a long period of time, make an effort to get meal vouchers as well as an hotel room, if required. Sometimes, they might even upgrade you to a more expensive level in service for your next flight if they require your seat urgently enough.

If you do not receive the items listed above, you must make an effort to get these items. Agents are trained to provide you with the lowest price first and gradually increase the price. If you're not satisfied with their offer , request more. If they refuse then you have to sit and see if someone else is willing to offer. If not, you could bargain again. When you receive an acceptable price: accept it! The longer you wait the more bargaining power you'll have in the majority of cases.

Skyscanner App

Financial Investing:

Overview

Disclaimer: Be aware when investing , and know that you are exposed to risks which could result in the loss of the entire amount you invested. Be wary that promise guaranteed income or claims that sound far too good to be true.

If you're concerned about conserving your capital, increasing the flow of cash, or comprehending the risks of investing, every traveler should be aware of the basics of investing. It is essential to be aware of the dangers associated with investing before you begin the process of creating your investment plan. We will provide you with a variety of elements to be aware of when you create the financial strategy.

Risks of Investment

How can you measure the risk? If you're a wanderer on the road What are the guidelines and risks that you must measure to ensure that you're on the right track and achieving your goals. When you're looking at the financial market or your company, you must to consider how much you're willing to risk. A single investment could result in an absolute loss. Making sure you are prepared for the ideal situation. The next step is to create an exit plan in the event that it's a short-term investment.

Time at Risk

If we are considering investing in the financial markets, it is important to think about your options. This will enable you to determine what kind of investment is possible. The money at risk may be at risk of penalties if it is taken out earlier than you expected. If you are using a trading platform like Think or Swim, Tradestation or Optionsxpress These platforms permit investors to invest in liquid assets like stocks (stocks) or mutual funds, and ETFs, or exchange-traded funds (ETFs). Insuring your capital for long durations of time could restrict your options as an online nomad. It is beneficial to have access to capital for those who are constantly looking to invest this money to invest in new ventures that could yield better yields. This brings us to the issue of opportunities cost.

Opportunity Cost

For investors, you should keep an eye on the possibility of investing in a different business or trade. Remember that market for finance are always volatile. Important factors to be considered include Net actual value (NPV) and the internal rate of returns (IRR) for any type of investment. If they are higher than zero , and the IRR is higher than the cost of opportunity an investment can be considered to be highly attractive. Consider these investment options against other possibilities and evaluate the better yields to arrive at an informed decision on the best place to put your money.

Transaction Fees

This is a subject that is rarely discussed. There is a cost that comes with each transaction. When buying an option, equity, home or a business there are transaction costs to be taken into consideration. If you buy or trade and sell businesses frequently it is important to be aware of the costs associated with these transactions and incorporate them into your model to gain an accurate understanding of actual return. Most of the time, returns from just one or two transactions will suffice to earn an adequate profit. If you're actively trading, the profits you earn from trades might be reduced by the number of transactions you conduct. Take note of the number of transactions you make as well as the price of every transaction. If you're seeking recommendations regarding trading software, we've got some on our website.

Volatility

We have already discussed that there are many aspects of investing (equities bonds, equity or alternative investments) which have specific factors that can affect the value of their base. In the case of equity investments, pay careful attention to the earnings per share, the price-to-equity ratio profitability ratios, as well as many other figures available on the finance section of numerous investment websites such as Yahoo Finance or Google Finance.

The factors in bonds are unique and can play an important role in the investment. Risk of interest rate as well as firm specific risk credit ratings, as well as the financials that underlie the issuer are all points of risk that can cause uncertainty. Keep an eye on budgets of the Federal Reserve and Federal budgets. You might want to consider bond mutual funds as a the diversification in your portfolio.

Alternative investments (real estate investment trusts, precious metals, limited partnerships, etc.) are subject to the risks they face. They are linked to equity markets or interest rates, as well as the legislation of Congress. In times of recession gold is a good investment extremely well, as do dollars-denominated assets (safe safe havens like euro, the dollar and Japanese Yuan).

Competition

As an online nomad and an opportunity seeker it is essential to stay informed of what your competition is up to. You've probably heard success stories of a variety of successful business-minded entrepreneurs. Has anyone followed up after their success? Amazon is the leader on the Internet in the retail sector. Did you realize that they're removing small , local stores and expanding into Wal-Mart's market? Generation X is used to buying on the internet. They are less likely to visit physical shops. All across America malls are empting out, and retail stores are going under. Sears, Macy's, and Best Buy are all in the zone of danger. This could eventually affect international retailers, as logistics in the developing countries continue to improve. Alibaba sells more goods every "Singles Day" than a whole year's worth of transactions made at Amazon and Amazon in the United States. All of their transactions happen on the internet.

It is important to remember that whatever the investment that you choose to make take into consideration the competitive environment. This is applicable to financial markets and also to the business world in general.

Market Size

In assessing the market for an investment there are many factors to take into consideration. This includes the growth in market that a potential investment has experienced in the past: is there a chance for expansion in the future in this industry?

What market is there and are there competitions in the field that are currently in play? What is their strategy?

Conclusion

It is the next thing to do: determine whether or not this kind of lifestyle is right for you. The thought of traveling and working from any place you'd like around the globe is an ideal dream that can be realized. It is possible to visit a variety of places and meet new people and work at a time that is the most convenient for you. There are a few issues must be considered prior to making the move as well as between finding jobs, finding locations which aren't costly to work from and much more it is not for everyone to like this lifestyle.

This book has taken time to understand what being a digital nomad about, as well as the steps you must to take to transform your dream into reality. If you're willing to invest the effort and time required to begin it can be a very appealing lifestyle to live. It isn't easy and isn't for everyone, but if are able to follow the steps which are provided in this guidebook and follow the steps, you'll be able to enjoy some amazing outcomes within a matter of minutes.

From learning about what is a digital nomad to finding the best locations in which you can stay with a minimum of money, and also to understand why having a second passport an excellent idea, and even some of your tax and banking concerns, this book will help you ensure you're ready to conquer the world and be the digital nomad you've always wanted to be.

If you're ready to step out into the world and create your own path and are willing to be entertained by various odd jobs online in order to find what you love and you're looking to explore the world and discover something completely new is the time to be ready to be an online nomad. If you're ready to begin this type of lifestyle, you should go through this guidebook!

www.ingramcontent.com/pod-product-compliance
Lightning Source LLC
Chambersburg PA
CBHW050402120526
44590CB00015B/1795